MW00991251

Your Inner Beauty

Your Inner Beauty

by Jill Freeman & Larry J. Freeman

New York • New Jersey

This 1996 edition is published by Park Lane Press,
a division of Random House Value Publishing, Inc.,
40 Engelhard Avenue, Avenel, New Jersey 07001.
http://www.randomhouse.com/

Park Lane Press and colophon are trademarks of
Random House Value Publishing, Inc.

Random House
New York • Toronto • London • Sydney • Auckland

Printed and bound in the United States of America

Library of Congress Cataloging-in-Publication Data

Freeman, Larry (Larry J.)
Your inner beauty / Larry & Jill Freeman.
p. cm.
Includes index.
ISBN 0-517-20029-5
1. Beauty, Personal. 2. Women—Health and hygiene. 3. Women—Mental health. I. Freeman, Jill, 1961- . II. Title.
RA778.F857 1996
613'.04244—dc20 96-33687
CIP

8 7 6 5 4 3 2 1

We dedicate this book to all the friends we've met through the years who have helped us discover that true beauty comes from within.

Jill Freeman
Larry J. Freeman

Acknowledgements • We wish to recognize and express much appreciation to Peter H. Engel for his faith in this project, and to Anne Colby, Jamie Mohn, Deborah McKibbin-Denson and Bruce Pierce for their work in helping to create this book.

Contents

Introduction • *Your Inner Beauty* is a beauty book that provides a greatly needed fresh perspective. Flip through any of the standard beauty bibles and what do you get? The same advice about caring for skin, hair, nails and fine-tuning your makeup and wardrobe. Some even cover proper eating, exercise, sleep and medical care problems. Of course, everyone knows that good health is an essential component of beauty.

But these books don't cover the most important beauty element of all: the secret beauty ingredient. It's an inner light, an irrepressible glow. Jackie Kennedy had it. So did Grace Kelly and Audrey Hepburn. Katherine Hepburn will never lose her true loveliness. And Mother Teresa, whose life has been filled with hardship and the observance of real misery and suffering, remains a deeply beautiful woman.

Your Inner Beauty describes what these women have in common that makes them so beautiful, and helps all women tap into their inner resources to achieve the same level of beauty for themselves. Not content to simply describe how to achieve real "inner beauty," this book offers the reader many interactive exercises, questionnaires, self-assessment charts and tracking forms to assist in the transformation process.

This is a unique beauty book. And while it also covers the more traditional beauty and health issues, its main thrust is to show women how they can enhance their appearance by tapping into their hidden inner beauty. What a major step forward! This concept redefines our definition of beauty. Not only that, it empowers women to take beauty out of the hands of others and into their own.

Inner beauty which emanates from a state of serenity, self-esteem, fulfillment and satisfaction illuminates any face, any figure, any age. It encompasses that spark, that glow, that air of supreme self-possession which we all recognize as true beauty. *Your Inner Beauty* is an empowering beauty book, essential reading for any woman who wants to look and feel more attractive. It shows every woman that she can awaken and reveal the beauty that is already within her.

—Jill Freeman & Larry J. Freeman

Chapter 1

Beauty Revealed

Real beauty does not reside on the surface; it emanates from a woman's inner being. Her appearance reflects who she is inside. Her actions are an extension of her being. She connects with her inner beauty not by trying to be beautiful, but by being more fully herself, her own person.

The truly beautiful woman possesses a spark of vitality that captivates our senses. You can see it in her eyes, in the way they sparkle when she talks. She has an appealing warmth, an unapologetic sensuality, a radiant glow. She is comfortable in her own skin. And that gives her an unshakable confidence—the most attractive feature of all.

When a woman is self-accepting, compassionate and serene, her physical flaws fade from view. Even a woman with less than perfect features will appear beautiful. But without the illuminating glow of inner beauty, the most attractive woman leaves us cold. It takes the transforming power of a woman's spirit to create the personal magnetism that is the hallmark of true beauty.

A woman in touch with her inner beauty knows that she is much more than the sum of her physical parts. She takes care of her physical appearance because she holds herself in regard. She chooses a hairstyle, makeup and clothing that reflect her personal style. But her beauty transcends fashion. It is uniquely and authentically her own—at its best, a soulful harmony of body, mind and spirit.

Beauty Inside Out

How do you get in touch with your inner beauty? You can't chase after it; you can only allow it to emerge. You invite it into your life by creating a vessel in which it can thrive.

Creating the right environment for your inner beauty means taking care of yourself physically, mentally and spiritually. You get the right amount of sleep, eat nutritious meals and get plenty of exercise. You establish good grooming habits. You nourish your mental life by exposing yourself to new ideas through reading, good conversation and cultural events. Finally, you cultivate your inner spirit by setting aside time each day for some kind of meditation, contemplation or worship.

Through it all, you pay attention to how you feel, what you like, what seems important and what doesn't. You begin to know yourself. You learn the things that give you joy and those that take it away. As you become more aware of what's going on inside you, everything in your life begins to fall into place.

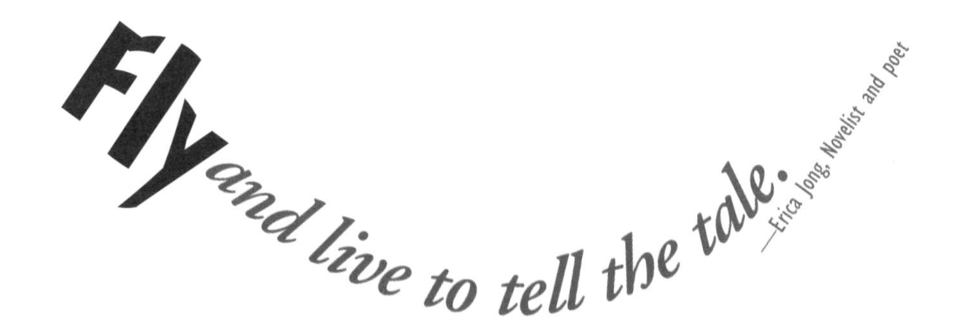

Take Stock

When asked to make a decision, do you tend to *think* things through before answering? Or do you go with whatever *feels* right at the time? Are you more likely to draw on past experiences or rely on a hunch? Do you consult other people or keep your thoughts to yourself?

Your responses to these questions can help reveal your personality, according to systems devised by psychologist Carl Jung and others. Which of these descriptions best fits you?

Thinker:	Tackles problems logically.
Feeler:	People-oriented and sympathetic.
Sensor:	Detail-oriented and practical.
Intuitor:	Imaginative, speculative, enjoys ideas.
Extrovert:	Energized by being with people. Talkative.
Introvert:	Recharged by time alone. May be shy or reserved.

Answering the following questions will help you identify your talents and goals.

What do you do well?______________________________

____

What do you most enjoy doing?__________________________

____

What things would you like to improve?____________________

____

What would you like to learn to do?______________________

____

What would you like to stop doing?_______________________

____

What are your big goals right now?_______________________

____

What lifetime goals would you like to achieve?_________________

____

Gold Getter

The day after speed skater Bonnie Blair claimed her sixth Olympic medal (five of them gold) at the 1994 Winter Olympics, someone asked her the secret of her success. Blair first named her easy grasp of technique, willingness to pay the price in training and consistent mental approach.

And what was the other key ingredient? "No matter what the competition or what the training," a determined Blair replied, "I've always tried to find a goal and better it."

Accept Yourself • It takes courage to begin the process. You must be willing to let go of worrying about what others think and instead learn to please yourself. You have to listen less to the outer voices—fashion magazines, television, peers—and more to your inner voice. And you must be prepared to appreciate the one-of-a-kind individual that you truly are: to like—not merely tolerate—your face, your hair, your legs and your figure; to enjoy your special accomplishments, talents and attributes; and then, finally, to be willing to express who you are to the world.

Consider three women, each with a physical feature that many would consider a flaw: Cindy Crawford with her trademark mole, Lauren Hutton with her gap-toothed smile, Barbra Streisand with her prominent nose. Each of these women took attributes that others might try to minimize or change and instead accepted them as part of themselves—even flaunted them in the public eye. They turned their *flaws* into their own unique signature, something that set them apart from the crowd. That's self-acceptance.

It's so easy to fall into the trap of measuring yourself against some outside standard and finding yourself lacking. But it's much healthier to learn to appreciate who and what you are.

Though we travel the world over to find the beautiful, we must carry it with us or we find it not.

—Ralph Waldo Emerson, Philosopher and author

When you accept yourself this way, you become more accepting of others. And that allows beauty to flourish in them as well.

Your Own Style

Women who are guided by a knowledge of their own inner identity do not feel they have to follow every fashion trend—they create their own. Katherine Hepburn is a perfect example. Her beauty transcended fashion, because it was uniquely and authentically her own. Tall, athletic and lanky—she quickly became known for her uniform of smart trousers and flats, which perfectly suited her body type and personality. She wore pants at a time when other women rarely did, but that was fine with her—she knew her style and stuck to it. She chose her own path in the fashion arena and in everything else she did!

Some people seem to have been born with a sense of what textures, lines, colors and shapes are just right for them. Others have to search awhile to find the look that says *me.* There is a wonderful freedom in finally discovering your own personal style.

There is no one else like you in the world. Why make yourself into a carbon copy of the latest flavor-of-the-month fashion model? What is the value of living your life to please other people? Free up your energy to be who you truly are and see what excitement that brings into your life!

Confidence Builders

When you find your confidence sagging, use these simple techniques to help bolster your self-esteem.

1. View your failures as useful learning experiences.

2. Trust in your ability to learn what you don't know when trying new things.

3. Pat yourself on the back when you do a good job.

4. When you make a mistake, look at it as a one-time event instead of singing the "I always get it wrong" refrain.

5. Affirm your confidence in yourself, even when you're experiencing doubts.

6. Visualize yourself doing exactly what you should be doing, and doing it well.

Plan Your Goals

If you suddenly learned that you had just five years to live, what would you most want to do with your time? And how would you spend it if you had just one year to live?

What are you waiting for? Take some time *now* to map out the goals you wish to accomplish in the near future and over your lifetime.

Long-range goals should include those skills, achievements and changes you would like to realize over the next five to ten years. These goals will provide an overall direction for your life and guide the course of your actions as you make decisions from day to day.

Medium-range goals are those activities, skills or qualities that you can prepare for now and attain in the next few years.

Short-range goals reflect your immediate concerns. Ideally, many short-term goals will help you accomplish those further down the road.

Perhaps one of your long-range career goals is to become a high-level manager in your company. Your short- and medium-range goals should help you build toward that end. A short-range goal might be to impress your boss with your skills and make her aware of your hopes for advancement. A medium-range goal might be to take the necessary training courses and get yourself on a management track. Your long-range goal of joining the management ranks then becomes just a matter of time.

Goals	Long-Range 5-10 Years	Medium-Range 1-5 Years	Short-Range Less than 1 year
Personal			
1.			
2.			
3.			
Career			
1.			
2.			
3.			
Health			
1.			
2.			
3.			

Goals	Long-Range 5-10 Years	Medium-Range 1-5 Years	Short-Range Less than 1 year
Family			
1.			
2.			
3.			
Spiritual			
1.			
2.			
3.			
Financial			
1.			
2.			
3.			
Social			
1.			
2.			
3.			

Of this lengthy list, what long-, medium- and short-range goals are most important to you now?

Long-Range Goals

1. ______

2. ______

3. ______

Medium-Range Goals

1. ______

2. ______

3. ______

Short-Range Goals

1. ______

2. ______

3. ______

What can you do today, tomorrow or next week to work toward one or more of these goals?

______

______

Confidence is Beautiful

Your physical appearance is greatly affected by your sense of yourself. As you become more confident and self-assured, your physical appearance begins to change dramatically. Your attractiveness increases as you become more vital, energetic and accessible. You develop a powerful sense of well-being that allows you to be more accepting of others.

A woman in touch with her inner beauty becomes what psychologist Abraham Maslow called a "self-actualizing" person—someone who is creative, spontaneous, expressive. She is inner-directed, meaning that she makes her decisions based on self-determined needs and goals, rather than those imposed from the outside. She feels fulfilled in whatever sphere of life that she chooses, confident about her relationship with the world and able to distinguish between the things that matter to her and those that don't. Because she supports and honors her inner being, she has more to offer the world.

When you are true to yourself in everything you do, you learn to trust your instincts and intuition to point you in the right direction. You begin to feel that everything is right in your world. You are in touch with your feminine strength and feel in control, confident and truly alive. A harmony pervades your life and your heart awakens to the beauty of life around you.

It is time for women to come out of hiding. Instead of asking, "Who, me?" it is time to say, "Here I am!"
—Susan Price, Psychotherapist and author

Express Yourself

Being in touch with your inner beauty does not mean becoming ladylike or passive in your approach to life. On the contrary, as you find out who you are, you become ever more involved. You discover a new energy to pursue your goals. You learn how to express your inner vision in the outside world.

"There is a vitality, a life force, an energy, a quickening that is translated through you into action, and because there is only one of you in all time, this expression is unique," says choreographer Martha Graham. "If you block it, it will never exist through any other medium and will be lost."

As you discover your unique talents and viewpoints, share them with others. Don't be content to blend into the background—speak up

How Assertive Are You?

In the spaces below, describe how you would respond to the following situations.

1. You learn from your male co-workers that they had drinks the previous night with your boss. While there, he solicited their input and they made an important decision that you should have been involved in.

I would ____

____

____

2. Your best friend has cancelled get-togethers with you three times this month, each time at the last minute.

I would ____

____

____

3. Your sister calls to ask if you can watch her children for the afternoon. You are working on an important project that needs to be finished by the end of the day.

I would ____

____

____

4. You're out to lunch with a group of people and you order a grilled ahi tuna sandwich. The waiter misunderstands and brings you a tuna salad sandwich instead.

I would ____

____

____

5. There's a party going on in the apartment next door. It's one in the morning and the music is still blasting through the walls, keeping you awake.

I would ____

____

____

Life is a daring adventure

and say what's on your mind! Develop your talents and expand your social network. Get involved with life and take on opportunities that seem right for you. Don't let your fears stand in the way of your self-expression and fulfillment.

By opening your heart to others and expressing the beauty of your inner self, you participate in the natural flow of life. As you give more of yourself to others, you find that others also want to give more of themselves to you.

Being Assertive

Assertiveness is the middle ground between passive do-nothingness and hostile aggression. It's being able to calmly assert your rights and express your feelings about a situation, even in the face of opposition. Being assertive does not mean acting in a way that alienates your boss, loses a friend or puts you in harm's way. It's staying in control of the situation and deciding what action would be in your best interest. What kind of choices did you make in response to the previous situations? Here are examples of assertive behavior.

1. Mention to your boss the conversation you had with your co-workers. Request that he or she include you in future decisions that involve you.

2. Raise the issue calmly with your friend, telling her that you don't appreciate her backing out at the last minute. Ask her to give you more notice if she needs to cancel, or to refrain from making commitments if she can't keep them.

3. Tell your sister that you would if you were free, but you can't today because of prior commitments. If you want to, offer to help out at another time when it's more convenient.

4. Call the waiter over and ask him to correct the situation.

5. Knock on your neighbor's door or call and tactfully ask them to turn down the stereo. If you think they might not appreciate

this approach and might cause problems, call the police instead and report the disturbance.

Trust Your Instincts

As you focus on your inner world, you will find yourself tuned into a source of wisdom that can help guide you in everything you do. Some call it intuition or a hunch; others refer to it as an inner compass or guide. It comes from the center of your being and often seems to be connected to a force greater than yourself. When you're *in the flow* of it, everything in your life seems to run more smoothly.

If you're not used to listening to this inner guide, it can take some practice to learn how to sort its message out from all the other thoughts that run through your head. It speaks to people in different ways: Some people hear an inner voice; others experience it as a feeling they can't explain. Some experience it as a sensation of *knowing* in their bodies; others *see* the right solution.

This is not the left-brain side of you that rationalizes, sorts, analyzes or lines up all the options into lists of pros and cons. Those skills are eminently useful for many things, but if you want to find the truth of a situation for yourself, it's often best to get out of your head and go deeper into your soul for the answer.

At the most basic level, your inner compass provides you with a survival instinct that keeps you out of dangerous situations. But it can be so much more. As you start paying greater attention to your inner guide, you will find it can help you in every situation you encounter, from the mundane to the life-changing. You will know which people to associate with, what job to accept, the best choice to make in any situation.

or nothing.

—Helen Keller, Author

When all of your decisions come from this unchanging center, your whole life achieves a kind of unity. You are tuned in to the infinite intelligence and in this way are connected to every other living organism. Just like every tree, flower and animal on earth, you fulfill your destiny by being exactly who and what you are.

Follow Your Bliss

When the late mythologist Joseph Campbell referred to the idea of living out one's dreams, he poetically referred to it as "following your bliss." He adapted this concept from an ancient Indian Sanskrit belief.

"If you follow your bliss," Campbell said in an interview with journalist Bill Moyers, "you put yourself on a kind of track that has been there all the while, waiting for you, and the life that you ought to be living is the one you are living. When you can see that, you begin to meet people who are in the field of your bliss, and they open the doors to you. Follow your bliss and don't be afraid, and doors will open where you didn't know they were going to be. If you are following your bliss, you are enjoying that refreshment, that 'eternal' life within you, all the time."

Does each of us really have a right path to follow? Does life really work that way? We all know those times when we are feeling *in sync*, when everything seems to go our way. At these times, we just seem to know exactly what to do next. We are listening to our inner guide.

If we listen closely enough, that guide will also reveal to us our previously unexplored desires and dreams. When we put ourselves on a path to pursue those dreams, our lives become more play than work. We are following our natural talents and affinities.

Many of us suppress our dreams when we think we need to be more practical. Sometimes that seems like our only choice. But don't block them out completely. Try them out a little bit at a time and enjoy the rewards they bring. Soon you may find that the only practical thing to do is to pursue your dreams wholeheartedly.

BEAUTY

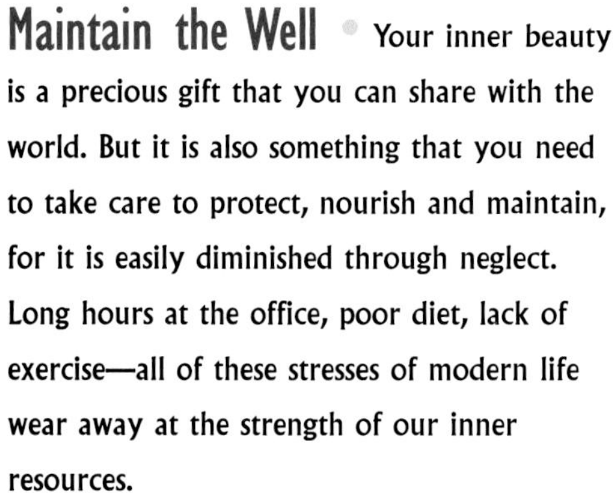

Maintain the Well

Your inner beauty is a precious gift that you can share with the world. But it is also something that you need to take care to protect, nourish and maintain, for it is easily diminished through neglect. Long hours at the office, poor diet, lack of exercise—all of these stresses of modern life wear away at the strength of our inner resources.

Think of your inner beauty as a deep well full of fresh, cool water. The water is always there, bubbling up from its source deep inside the earth. But if you forget to maintain the well and it falls into disrepair, you will have no way to gather the water. To enjoy and experience your inner beauty—to draw on the cool, refreshing water—you must take good care of your body, mind and spirit.

Follow this journey to your inner self. It will be time well spent.

Nobody can make you feel inferior without your consent.

—Eleanor Roosevelt, Former First Lady

Chapter 2

Sleep & Dreams

"Things will look better in the morning." How many times have we heard those words? When we are physically or emotionally spent, it is often hard to believe anything could ever look better. But a good night's sleep does indeed cure many ills. After a night of restful slumber, we wake up with a fresh outlook on a situation that just ten hours earlier looked bleak and hopeless.

With our busy lives, it's tempting to let our waking hours encroach upon our dream time, stealing away an hour here and a half-hour there. Sleep seems like wasted time, hours in which we aren't getting anything done.

Good health and a positive outlook depend on our getting the sleep we need. During sleep our metabolism shifts into a lower gear, giving us needed rest to prepare for the coming day. At the same time, our minds are busy processing the day's experiences in our dreams: committing important ideas to memory, recasting negative experiences into a more positive light and tossing out the information we don't need.

How important is sleep to our functioning? We reduce our daytime alertness by cheating ourselves out of just an hour or two of sleep every night. Skip one night of sleep, and we lose spontaneity and creativity. Miss two nights of sleep, and our perception, memory and judgment are significantly impaired.

The average person sleeps seven to nine hours, but anything from four to twelve hours a night may be normal. Let your sleep be guided by your body's own signals. How long do you typically sleep when you don't have to get up at a specific time? How many hours of shut-eye do you need before you feel and look rested? If you're feeling run-down, give yourself some extra sleep—this is what's popularly referred to as *beauty sleep.* That investment of an extra hour or two will help you avoid illness and reduce stress. A good night's sleep is one luxury that's absolutely free.

Easy Sleep • For the millions who suffer from insomnia, getting to bed is not a problem—but getting to sleep is. If you're having trouble falling asleep, here are some things you can do to hasten slumber.

Start by getting your eating and exercise habits in order. Watch your intake of caffeine during the day, and limit the caffeine drinks to the morning hours. Eat and drink lightly in the evening, and stay away from alcohol late at night. If you're hungry before bedtime, have a light snack—a glass of milk or a banana—both foods are high in tryptophan, which promotes sleepiness.

Sometimes the most urgent and vital thing you can possibly do is take a complete rest.

—Ashleigh Brilliant, Illustrator and humorist

Not getting enough exercise during the day can inhibit sleep, so be sure to get some type of physical activity each day—even if it's just a brisk walk at lunch time. But avoid strenuous exercise up to three hours before bedtime.

Is your room cluttered with paperwork from the office, sewing projects to finish, bills waiting to be paid? Banish all these anxiety-inducing piles to another room. Make your bedroom a restful, rejuvenating place. Install dark shades or heavy drapes or use a sleep mask to block out light that can interfere with sleep. If the din from street traffic or a snoring partner is keeping you awake, get a white-noise machine or a small fan to mask the noise or earplugs to block it out. If your bedroom is decorated in high-energy reds and stimulating patterns, you may want to tone down the visual noise. Light blue is the most popular bedroom color, because of its restful properties. White is another refreshing color, especially in bedding. Make sure your bed is comfortable, with a high-quality mattress, mattress pad, pillows and clean cotton sheets. Stock your night table with fragrant oils and incense in sleep-inducing scents such as lavender, ylang-ylang, sandalwood and rose.

> We need time to dream, time to remember and time to reach the infinite. Time to be.
> —Gladys Taber, Writer

When it's time for bed, establish rituals that signal to your body that it's time to wind down. Get into bed early, put on some relaxing music and turn down the lights. Stay away from the violence-laden TV news programs and chatty talk shows. Instead, relax your body and mind with deep breathing and other exercises described in the relaxation chapter. Satisfying sex can be another good natural relaxant. If after all of this you still find yourself tossing and turning, get out of bed and do something else until you're ready to nod off. No matter what time you fall asleep, get out of bed at the same time every morning to help maintain a routine.

Nap Time • When it comes to napping, the world divides into two kinds of people: Those who nap and those who don't. Opinions on the benefits of napping are strongly divided. Some people swear they cannot nap—either they can't fall asleep in the daytime or they don't want to. Others look forward to their naps with great pleasure, particularly on weekend days after a strenuous week or while on vacation.

Restless Nights

If you're getting enough sleep, eating well and exercising regularly, yet are still chronically tired, it's possible you have a sleep disorder and need to contact

your physician for treatment. There are more than eighty different kinds of sleep disorders. Those who suffer from sleep apnea, one common sleep disturbance, have trouble breathing during the night. (They can be identified by their tell-tale snore.) Every time sleep apnea sufferers' air passages get blocked, they stop breathing for a moment, which interrupts their sleep. In the morning, they are still tired but have no memory of having woken up during the night.

A nap can be a quick pick-me-up in a long day, or just a way to relax and enjoy one's leisure time.

Some sleep experts say mid-afternoon is a natural time for a nap, since energy levels are lowest at this time of day. In some countries with warm southern climates, it has been the custom to take an afternoon rest during the hottest part of the day, after a large mid-day meal. Thus refreshed, work and other activities then resume in the late afternoon.

Perhaps our 3 p.m. coffee break would be better replaced by a short snooze break. Most people may not be able to get away with a nap at their desks, but there are other possibilities. If your company has a lounge area or if there is a nice private outdoor area nearby, you can shut your eyes for a few minutes at lunch or in mid-afternoon. You can take a short nap after you get home from work to refresh yourself for the evening. At home or on vacation, you'll find numerous places to enjoy a nap: in a hammock on the lawn or porch, on the couch, in bed, by the pool, at the beach, on the grass at the park or on a massage table at a spa.

Limit nap duration to between thirty minutes and an hour. Much more time spent napping can interfere with your ability to sleep at night.

Melatonin Madness • Ever since the word went out on the effectiveness of melatonin as a sleep aid, sales of the dietary supplement have gone through the roof. While sleeping pills and alcohol are to be avoided as sleep enhancers (they interfere with dreaming so you don't get a complete rest), melatonin, the so-called natural sleeping pill, so far appears to be safe—but the verdict is still out.

Melatonin is a hormone we produce naturally. Secreted from the pea-sized pineal gland in the front of the brain, melatonin keeps us in sync with the rhythms of the day. When darkness falls, the gland starts pumping melatonin. In response, our body temperature falls and our metabolism slows to prepare us for sleep. In the morning, when light hits the retina, melatonin secretion tapers off, allowing us to awaken. When we are children, melatonin production is in full swing, but as we get older, the amount we secrete declines.

The sleep-impaired are lining up to buy the hormone in pill form. Although it's sold in doses of one milligram or more, as little as a tenth of a milligram can make dozing off easier. (Our pineal glands circulate just a third of a milligram at one time.) Melatonin is especially popular with frequent travelers who jet between time zones. Small doses of the hormone shift the body's clock forward or backward. If you take it in the late afternoon, it simulates an earlier sunset; if you take it in the morning, your clock moves backward as if the night lasted longer.

Although melatonin has been studied since 1980, the long-term repercussions of fooling with the body's time clock are not yet known. So far, it appears safe, at least for short-term use. Some side effects—headaches, nausea, chronic grogginess—have been reported. And because melatonin is sold as a dietary supplement (rather than a drug,) production is not monitored and contamination is always a possibility.

You should avoid taking melatonin if you are pregnant or nursing, trying to get pregnant (in large doses it apparently suppresses ovulation) or have severe allergies, an auto-immune disease, immune-system cancer or depression. Children don't need it because they produce plenty themselves.

Time Travelers • When you fly long distances across time zones, your body continues to operate on the rhythms established at home. While melatonin pills appear to be a very effective cure for jet lag, not everyone is comfortable taking a pill. Here are some ways to help your body adjust:

- Begin changing your bedtime three nights before your trip. If you're traveling east to west, go to bed one hour later for every time zone you will cross. If you're traveling west to east, go to bed one hour earlier for every time zone change.
- Drink plenty of water and juice before and during your flight. Keep alcohol to a minimum and eat moderately.
- After you arrive, spend at least one hour in daylight for every time zone you have crossed. Take walks in the morning to get used to the earlier light when flying east, and in the afternoon when flying west.
- Avoid napping. Try to go to bed at a reasonable time in the evening instead, and allow plenty of time for sleep.

Dreams Explained • We all dream, whether we remember our dreams or not. If we are kept from dreaming, either because of sleep deprivation or substance abuse, our mental health suffers. Dreams help us make connections, process emotions and put ideas in their place. We need dreams to fix information in our minds. Our dreaming minds work on problems, transferring the information from short-term to long-term memory up to a week after we receive it.

In 1952 a University of Chicago graduate student measured the brain waves of his sleeping son and discovered that certain brain rhythms correspond with rapid eye movements under the eyelids. This period of deep sleep became known as REM (rapid eye movement) sleep, and it is the time when most dreaming occurs.

Every night when we fall asleep, we enter a sleep cycle comprised of four levels of sleep, each level distinguished by successively slower brain rhythms. After we pass through the fourth and last level, we ascend back up to the first level, where we begin to dream. We experience four to seven of these cycles per night. Dreaming occurs in the first level of every cycle except the initial one.

We spend about two hours dreaming each night and have an average of four to five dreams. A dream can be from two minutes to an hour long, but the typical dream clocks in at fifteen to twenty minutes.

The first dream of the evening is often a replaying of events and preoccupations of the previous day, recast into a story our unconscious mind prefers. These are literal and non-symbolic dreams that can be taken at face value. But each successive dream takes us deeper into the unconscious, often building upon stories and symbols established in previous dreams. The last dream of the night, the one we most often remember, comes from the deepest part of our unconscious.

Dreamers in History • Perhaps because they are so mysterious, vivid and fanciful, we have always been fascinated by dreams. No one knows for sure what their significance is because dreams speak to us in symbolic language. But from the beginning of history, people have believed that dreams convey important information. The challenge is to decipher their meaning.

Many ancient peoples thought the future was prophesied through dreams. One of the most famous Bible stories tells of Joseph, sold into slavery in Egypt, who correctly interpreted the dream of the pharaoh and prophesied seven years of prosperity and seven years of drought. With his early warning of famine ahead, Egypt was able to survive and thrive, and Joseph became prime minister.

Aristotle believed that dreams can tip us off to illnesses in the body. Today, scientists are studying that same possibility. Dream researchers have documented cases where dreams have predicted future illnesses and brought to light medical problems that were not previously known.

Numerous artists, writers and musicians have had inspiration for their work through dreams. A dream inspired Robert Louis Stevenson's story *The Strange Case of Dr. Jekyll and Mr. Hyde.* Samuel Coleridge wrote the poem "Kubla Khan" in a dream. Paul McCartney woke up with the music to "Yesterday" running through his head.

Dreams have also played a role in science and industry. The ground-breaking discovery of the molecular structure of the benzene ring came to German chemist Friedrich Kekulé von Stradonitz in a dream. While working on the problem, Kekulé fell asleep and dreamed of molecules dancing around, then joining together like a snake catching its tail.

The design for the modern sewing machine was perfected when the inventor dreamed that he was captured by savages who were about to execute him with spears that had eye-shaped holes near the tips.

All this points out the humor that our unconscious minds often use to communicate. Dreams are known to be rich with visual jokes and wordplay that often provide a key to their meaning. Imagery that appears ridiculous on its face may make sense when examined in the context of what is going on during our waking hours.

In this century, Sigmund Freud and his student Carl Jung have led the study of dream interpretation. Freud hypothesized that dreams bring messages from the unconscious mind. Perhaps because he lived during the repressive Victorian period, he interpreted most dream symbols in terms of sexual wishes and needs. Carl Jung came up with a much broader theory about dream symbols that is the model for what we believe today.

Some dreams, Jung said, draw upon information contained in the *personal unconscious*—all of the forgotten or repressed experiences we have felt, thought and subliminally perceived. The precise meaning of the symbols that appear in these dreams depends on the psychology and history of the

Only a Dream

While you were dreaming, have you ever suddenly been aware that "this is only a dream"? Being aware in a dream that you are having a dream and then using that awareness to shape and direct it is called *lucid dreaming.*

You can use lucid dreaming to pull yourself out of a nightmare by confronting whatever is frightening you instead of running away from it. Often by taking the power away from our dreamtime *monsters,* we subsequently put to rest the emotions that caused the troubling dream. You can take charge of your dreams and write in the happy ending you prefer.

dreamer. Often they bring to light emotions of which we were unaware or provide a solution to a problem we have been grappling with during our waking hours.

There are also higher-level dreams that impart important life wisdom to us. In these dreams we access the *collective unconscious*—the past experiences and memories of all of humanity that shape our instinctive thoughts and behavior. These dreams can be identified by the appearance of universal archetypes: the Hero or Heroine, representing our brave, strong self, who is often depicted embarking on an important journey or quest; the Divine Child, who embodies our true, complete self and sometimes symbolizes a rebirth; the Great Mother, a female figure, who can represent many qualities including growth, fertility, virginity, spirituality, feminine power, seductiveness and jealousy; the Father, or another authority figure, who can be either a source of primary wisdom and strength or a tyrant and destroyer.

Other archetypes include: the Animus, the male aspect inside every woman, who might appear in a dream as a man exhibiting *masculine* qualities the woman needs to integrate within herself; the Anima, the female aspect of the male psyche, who might appear as a woman in a man's dream representing his *feminine* qualities; the Persona, the self or *mask* we present to the world; and the Shadow, the repressed, primitive side of ourselves who appears as a figure reminding us of things we prefer not to see, yet need to accept.

The more you discover about yourself, the more you want to live what you're discovering.
—Julia Boyd, Writer

Interpreting Dreams • The benefits you get from dreaming do not depend on remembering your dreams. But you can gain greater access to your inner life by unlocking the meaning of symbols and stories expressed in your dreams. Often emotions and perceptions simmer in the unconscious and only bubble up during dream time. If you are working on a problem, you can use your dream life to gain the information you need.

The best way to do that is to keep a dream journal. Use the form at the end of this chapter as a guide. When you wake up in the morning, lie in bed and focus on the dream images you remember. Write them down right away if you can. Jot down a story line, the people that appeared in your dreams, the scenery, important or nonsensical details that stood out or called attention to themselves and emotions you felt during the dream and upon waking.

Start by looking at possible connections between recent events and the events in your dream. Was your mind replaying something that happened to you recently? If the imagery in the dream goes beyond a literal reading, start by looking at what the dream images mean to you and the emotions they conjure up. Without analyzing too much, what is your initial association with these people, stories, settings and events? After you let your own associations drift to the surface, you may want to look through dream dictionaries to find out what universal or archetypal meanings are associated with the dream images. Do they add another layer of meaning, or are they just a distraction from what the images really mean to you?

For example, parties are usually considered happy celebratory events. If for you parties mean something less positive and your dream recalls those emotions, you should value your own associations over the universal symbol. On the other hand, your mind may be pointing out the contrast between what society says and what you feel about an event in your life.

Many universal dream symbols make sense intuitively: Climbing a mountain or a ladder can represent striving toward a goal or a higher state of being. It can also mean the dreamer is in a precarious state. Houses and cars are both common images for the self. Body parts appearing in a dream can indicate the parts of the body which have problems or need to be put to better use. Oceans often symbolize consciousness or an emotional state. Shopping may represent a search for new attitudes and beliefs, or a need to make choices.

Were there any transitions in the dream—a house changing into a car or a person turning into someone else? These can call attention to situations in our lives that are changing or need to change. If you dream that you turn into a bird, for example, it may indicate a new freedom in your life or a desire to explore new territory.

Finally, look at recurring motifs. These may indicate important themes in your life, or may be your mind's way of trying to draw attention to an area of your life that you are ignoring.

The more we pay attention to our dreams, the more skilled we will become at understanding their language. Soon, dreams will alert us when we're not taking care of ourselves and need to choose another course of action. They will connect us to the child in each of us and to the magic of our imaginations. They will remind us of the hopes we have for the future, which we may not allow ourselves in our waking lives. Dreams can become a nighttime *window* into the world of our souls, the place where inner beauty begins.

Dream Diary

Before you go to bed at night, give yourself the positive suggestion that you will remember what you dream that night. Keep a pad of paper or a dream journal and a pen by your bed so you can record your dreams as soon as you wake up. Get as much sleep as you need.

In the morning, before you open your eyes or move around, think about the dream images that were with you upon waking. Fix on a key image or replay the dream in your mind, going through it from beginning to end, noting important details. Then write it down. If you're pressed for time, just record a key image or summary of a scene. Later, when you have the time, you can go back and fill in the rest of your dream notes.

Were there any details in the dream that seemed to be emphasized? Something that was so nonsensical it stood out? Sometimes these are the most important details—the key that unlocks the dream's meaning.

Date of Dream: ______________________________

Description of Dream Events: ______________________________

____

____

____

____

____

____

Settings Where the Dream Occurred: ______________________________

____

____

____

People Who Appeared in the Dream: ______________________________

____

____

____

Important Details: ______

Nonsensical Elements or Events: ______

Emotions Felt in the Dream and Upon Waking: ______

Transformations: ______

Possible Symbols or Wordplay: ______

Recent Waking Concerns: ______

Possible Dream Meanings: ______

Chapter 3

Eating well

We have been through papaya, high-protein and milkshake diets. We have suffered through countless frozen diet dinners with the taste and consistency of cardboard. We have signed our paychecks over to weight-loss centers and stocked our cupboards with sugar- and fat-free foods. All in the name of staying fit.

In the midst of this diet madness, it is easy to lose track of the real importance of food. Food provides the fuel we need to get through the day. When we eat a baked potato or a Caesar salad, our bodies convert the sugar, starch, fat and protein in it into energy

(measured in calories) that we use or store. We also absorb the vitamins and minerals that the food contains and keep what we need for ourselves.

It is at this point where many weight-loss diets fail. Either they don't provide enough calories to keep us going (we must consume a minimum of ten calories for every pound of our ideal body weight each day to keep our metabolisms functioning at a normal rate), or they don't contain the nutrients we need to stay healthy.

Diets for most people mean deprivation and self-punishment, states no healthy individual can stand for very long. We need pleasure to survive and thrive, and food provides it in spades. We delight in the smell of good cooking, the taste and feel of it in our mouths and the ritual of breaking bread with friends and family. Any diet that does not allow for these simple pleasures is not going to be followed for very long.

But with so much pressure today to stay thin, the promise of quick weight loss is tempting. And so we diet. Invariably, though, when the diet's over and we resume our old eating habits, the weight returns. And then it's time for another diet. However, the more we diet, the less effective diets become. Our bodies think they have to store up extra energy to protect us from starvation, so our metabolisms slow down, as if we were going

Ideal Weight Ranges for Women

Height	Weight	Height	Weight	Height	Weight
5'0"	97-118	5'4"	111-132	5'9"	129-151
5'1"	101-121	5'5"	114-135	5'10"	132-156
5'2"	104-125	5'6"	118-139	5'11"	136-161
5'3"	107-128	5'7"	121-142	6'0"	140-166
		5'8"	125-146		

into hibernation. Eventually we find we're eating almost nothing at all, but not losing weight. It's a destructive cycle that can lead to anorexia or bulimia, serious diseases that can be life threatening and currently afflict an estimated eight million Americans, most of them women.

Once the cycle begins, it's hard to break. But break it we must. Not necessarily by eating less, but by eating better: more complex carbohydrates, less fat and sugar. Complex carbohydrates are the closest thing to a miracle food that nature offers. Whether you are trying to lose weight or not, complex carbohydrates are the foods you should be eating to maintain good health for the rest of your life.

Complex Carbohydrates • Carbohydrates come in two forms: simple and complex. Simple carbohydrates are found in fruit (fructose) and refined sugar (sucrose). They are good for instant energy, but the body burns them off quickly. Complex carbohydrates are strands of simple sugars found in rice, potatoes, grains, vegetables and legumes. They take longer to digest and provide more steady, long-lasting energy.

Carbohydrates are a great food for those who want to lose weight for several reasons. Your body immediately converts carbohydrates into glucose for fuel and only stores those calories

Model Thin

Do you ever find yourself feeling fat after paging through fashion magazines or watching TV? Consider this: A generation ago, fashion models weighed 8 percent less than the average woman. Today they weigh 23 percent less. The average model, dancer and actress is thinner than 95 percent of *all* women.

Love yourself first and everything else falls into line.

—Lucille Ball, Actor

Feel-Good Foods

Looking for low calorie, lowfat foods to give you energy and fill you up? You won't go wrong with these, as long as you don't add high-fat spreads and toppings.

Whole-Grain Breads
Pita Bread
Bagels
Tortillas
Rice
Pasta
Barley
Potatoes
Couscous
Graham Crackers
Animal Crackers
Pretzels
Oatmeal
Cereals, Lowfat
Muffins, Lowfat
Pancakes
Waffles
Legumes (Peas, Beans and Lentils)
Tofu
Vegetables

it doesn't need for energy. In contrast, it stores virtually all fat calories immediately into your fat cells. Also, when the body stores the energy of carbohydrates, it takes 23 percent of its calories to convert it to storage as body fat. Converting the fat you eat into body fat uses up only 3 percent of its calories.

There's more. You can eat more than twice as much with a diet made up of carbohydrates as one made up of fat. Why? Each gram of carbohydrate contains just four calories, while every gram of fat contains nine.

Carbohydrates also increase your metabolic rate, whereas fats do not. So your body burns off calories faster when carbohydrates make up the majority of your meals.

In simple terms, it's much easier to become fat by eating fat than it is by eating carbohydrates. You can eat more, weigh less and have more energy to get through the day with a diet high in carbohydrates.

Nutritional Needs • What is an ideal diet for good health? One that's built around whole grains and cereals, brown

It is never too late
—in fiction or in life—
to revise.

—Nancy Thayer, Writer

Food Diary

Do you really know how much you eat each day? Use this food diary to get an accurate picture of your eating habits. For each category of food, divide the total servings by three to get your daily average. Then compare your consumption to the ideal.

FOOD	Day one servings	Day two servings	Day three servings	Servings per day	Average ideal servings per day
Grains, breads, cereal, rice, pasta serving = 1 slice bread, $\frac{1}{2}$ cup cereal, rice or pasta					6-11
Vegetables serving = $\frac{1}{2}$ cup cooked, 1 cup raw, leafy					3-5
Fruits serving = 1 apple, $\frac{3}{4}$ cup juice					2-4
Legumes, beans, fish, poultry, eggs, meat, nuts serving = $\frac{1}{2}$ cup cooked beans, 2-3 oz. lean meat, 1 egg					2-3
Milk, cheese, yogurt (nonfat or lowfat) serving = 1 cup milk, $1\frac{1}{2}$-2 oz. cheese					2-4
Fats, sweets, alcohol serving = 1 tbs. oil, 2 tbs. salad dressing, 1 glass wine					Minimal

rice, raw or steamed vegetables, legumes, nuts, seeds and fruits. If you are eating a variety of foods from these groups, you can get all the nutrients you need.

Is it really safe to be a vegetarian? Yes, as long as you eat the right foods. You get plenty of protein when you combine legumes, such as peas, lentils and beans, with grains, such as rice, corn and wheat. You can satisfy your need for iron—a nutrient meat provides—by eating whole grains and green vegetables.

Not everyone wants to be a vegetarian; some people still prefer to eat meat. Others skip the red meat but eat poultry or fish. Still others abstain from flesh products, but eat dairy products and eggs. The choice is yours. But if you do eat meat, poultry and fish, keep the servings to three to four ounces a day. Choose fish before poultry and skinless poultry before meat, and limit your egg consumption to just a few a week. (You can also eat egg-white omelets to eliminate the fat entirely.) Stay away from processed luncheon meats.

You may or may not want to include milk in your diet. Milk is an excellent source of calcium, a nutrient women need to prevent osteoporosis, but many people develop an intolerance for milk as adults. If milk isn't for you, you might try a lactose-free substitute. You can also substitute yogurt, which is often easier to digest than milk. Yogurt, if it contains active cultures, also has the added benefit of preventing vaginal yeast infections. Be sure to buy nonfat or lowfat dairy products. If you choose to avoid dairy entirely, you can

Life itself is the proper binge.

—Julia Child, Chef, author and television personality

also get calcium in fish, shellfish and dark green vegetables (other than spinach).

How much fat do you need in your diet? The American Medical Association says it should be about 30 percent of your daily calories. But many nutritionists recommend a much lower consumption—just 10 to 20 percent of your daily diet. The American Cancer Society recommends that your daily caloric intake be comprised of 20 to 25 percent fat, 15 percent protein and 60 percent carbohydrate to maintain optimum health.

You are the best judge of your needs. Do you get a lot of strenuous physical exercise? Do you have a metabolism that burns energy fast? Then you can tolerate more fat. If you're getting just a moderate amount of exercise each day and have a slower metabolism, you'll need less fat each day to maintain your ideal weight. To keep your cholesterol level down, use monounsaturated and cold-pressed vegetable oils and watch the butter.

Be careful not to fall into the trap of loading up on "fat-free" prepared snacks and desserts that are high in sugar, contain very few nutrients and are not very satisfying. White flour, white rice, refined sugar, alcohol and caffeine drinks should be kept to a minimum because they have little or no nutritional value. Skip the diet sodas, and drink water instead. Buy as many organically grown foods as possible, rather than those treated with potentially harmful chemicals, growth hormones and additives.

Does this recipe for eating sound strict and fun-free? It doesn't have to be. Tons of cookbooks offer healthful, flavorful recipes that center on vegetables, fruits and grains. You can find better prepared foods today, especially at health food stores and restaurants. It takes a little work to change your eating practices. But lighter, healthier food tastes better once you get used to it. And the result of this kind of eating is that you will feel more energetic and look better too.

Chocolate Cure

There is one not-so-healthy food that tempts even the most well-intentioned healthy eater: chocolate. Its rich flavor, sensuous mouth feel and association with love make it hard to resist. But there may be chemical reasons behind our cravings for it too. Chocolate stimulates our bodies to produce endorphins, a feel-good chemical that anesthetizes

us against pain. Chocolate is also thought to trigger our bodies to produce serotonin, a hormone that calms and relaxes us, and theobromine, which aids digestion. It also contains a little caffeine, a stimulant.

These things may explain why some women feel chocolate cravings right before their period—a time when serotonin levels are lower and PMS discomfort is in full swing.

The problem for many is that chocolate candy is loaded with fat. What do you do to satisfy your chocolate cravings without tipping the scales? Make your own hot cocoa with nonfat milk, or have a serving of a fat-free chocolate dessert.

Vitamins & Minerals

The best way to get your nutrients is by eating a wide variety of foods. Here are the vitamins and minerals your body needs to function well and prevent disease. Are you getting everything you need? Check to see what foods may be missing in your diet. If there are significant gaps, or if you want the assurance that you're getting everything you need, you may want to consider a vitamin and mineral supplement.

Nutrient:	Sources:	Body processes it aids:	Organs/systems affected:
Vitamin A (retinol, carotene)	fish oils, milk, liver, egg yolks, green and yellow vegetables, orange and yellow fruits	N/A	hair, skin, teeth, gums, eyes, bones, blood cells, immune system
Vitamin B_1 (thiamine)	whole grains, legumes, oatmeal, milk, nuts, lentils, seeds, eggs	metabolism of complex carbohydrates, energy production	N/A
Vitamin B_2 (riboflavin)	dairy products, cereals, meat, leafy greens, peas, beans, eggs, wheat germ	N/A	liver
Vitamin B_3 (niacin)	whole grains, dairy products, meat, fish, brewer's yeast, green vegetables, nuts, eggs	metabolism of carbohydrates, reduction of fats in blood	N/A
Vitamin B_5 (pantothenic acid)	dairy products, eggs, cereals, meat, brewer's yeast, green vegetables, mushrooms	metabolism of carbohydrates, fats, amino acids	adrenal glands, immune system
Vitamin B_6 (pyridoxine)	fish, meat, egg yolks, whole grains, nuts, seeds, green vegetables, brewer's yeast, bananas, avocados, molasses, mushrooms	metabolism of proteins, amino acids, sugars, fatty acids, minerals	red blood cells, antibodies, hormones, enzymes
Vitamin B_{12} (cyanocobalamin)	meat, fish, eggs, dairy products, bean sprouts	metabolism of iron	blood cells, nervous system
Vitamin C (ascorbic acid)	fresh fruit, fresh vegetables, potatoes	protection from infections, viruses, toxins, drugs, allergies, antioxidation	skin, bones, muscles
Vitamin D	dairy products, eggs, fish oil	N/A	bones, teeth
Vitamin E	nuts, seeds, eggs, dairy products, whole grains, wheat germ, unrefined oils, leafy vegetables, avocados	metabolism of essential fatty acids, slowdown of aging, iron absorption, antioxidation	red blood cells, circulatory system, cells
Vitamin K	green vegetables, dairy products, molasses, apricots, whole grains, cod liver oil, sunflower oil	blood clotting	N/A

Nutrient:	Sources:	Body processes it aids:	Organs/systems affected:
Folic acid	brewer's yeast, green vegetables, eggs, whole grains, meat, nuts, dairy products	metabolism of sugar, amino acids	antibodies, red blood cells, nervous system
Sodium	salt, vegetables	fluid balance, blood pressure	nerves, muscles
Calcium	dairy products, green vegetables, eggs, nuts, seeds, dried fruit, soy beans, fish, cereals	N/A	bones, teeth, heart, blood, nerves, muscles
Iron	egg yolks, liver, meat, molasses, soy beans, whole grains, green vegetables, fish, dried fruits, cocoa, wine	oxygen transfer in the blood, cellular respiration, energy production	N/A
Magnesium	green vegetables, nuts, seeds, whole grains, dairy products, eggs, seafood	energy production	enzymes, nerves, muscles, bones, teeth
Phosphorus	whole grains, seeds, nuts, meat, fish, eggs	metabolism of vitamins	bones, heart, kidney, nerves
Potassium	fresh fruit, fresh vegetables, whole grains, nuts, soy beans, seafood	N/A	nerves, muscles, blood
Copper	green vegetables, liver, seafood, whole grains	antioxidation, iron absorption	nerves, enzymes, brain, bones, connective tissue
Zinc	oysters, herring, yeast, liver, eggs, beef, peas, seeds, fruit, vegetables, nuts, poultry, shellfish	metabolism of protein, protection against free-radical damage	enzymes, immune system, hormones, bones, joints
Cobalt	brewer's yeast, fruit, vegetables, whole grains, nuts	copper absorption, magnesium and sugar metabolism	N/A
Manganese	green vegetables, seeds, whole grains, brewer's yeast, eggs, fruit, tea	energy metabolism	bones, thyroid, nervous and reproductive systems
Iodine	vegetables, fruits, seafood, garlic, parsley, iodized salt	physical and mental development	thyroid, metabolism
Chromium	fruit, vegetables, meat, molasses, whole grains, wheat germ, brewer's yeast	fat and carbohydrate metabolism, energy production	N/A
Selenium	garlic, whole grains, eggs, meat, brewer's yeast	antioxidation	liver, connective tissues, sex hormones

Diet Success

Dieters most likely to keep the pounds off for good are those who design their own weight-loss programs rather than those who follow someone else's programs, according to a University of California at Davis study. Of those who lost weight and kept it off, 73 percent developed their own plans, compared to 20 percent who attended Weight Watchers or a similar program.

Some of the reasons for their success? Ninety percent designed a program that had them exercising at least thirty minutes, three times a week. Successful dieters were more likely to include favorite foods on their menus and set modest, attainable goals. And rather than overeat when they experienced stress, they were more likely to talk to a friend or a counselor.

Restaurant Smarts • When you're trying to improve your eating habits, restaurant food can prove a challenge. Many times the portions are two or three times the size you would normally prepare for yourself. It's hard to tell exactly how much oil or butter has been used in the dish. And since you're staying at the table longer than you might at home and the food is there in front of you, you have a greater tendency to eat more than you should. But there are ways around these potential pitfalls.

First, choose restaurants that have an enlightened attitude about healthy cooking. A growing number of restaurants today are focusing their menus on tasty, lowfat cooking. Give them your business!

Make butter-laden sauces a rare treat, and choose items that are fresh, baked, steamed or broiled. Ask for salad dressing on the side, or choose one low in oil. Skip the butter on the bread unless it's your favorite indulgence. Don't automatically order dessert. If you want something sweet, consider a fruit dish or sorbet. For that occasional rich indulgence, split it with your companion so you get a taste of it in moderation.

If a restaurant serves big portions, consider sharing a dish with your dinner companion and then each ordering a separate soup or salad. Often this is enough for a generous meal for both of you. Otherwise, plan to take some of the meal home with you if it's too much food for one sitting. When your dish arrives, decide right away how much of it you're going to eat. Separate it on the plate or order a doggie bag right away.

Most important to remember, eat mindfully. Savor the tastes and textures of each dish. Give your full attention to the meal. Then when you've finished, you'll know you've really eaten!

One cannot
think well,
love well,
sleep well,
if one has not
dined well.

—Virginia Woolf, Novelist

Chapter 4

Keeping Fit

We need to exercise to stay in shape. But the benefits of a regular workout go beyond toned triceps and a tighter gluteus maximus. Our bodies are made to move! We are like perpetual motion machines, with our every movement triggering an important physical function. Stop the motion, and the whole system slowly comes to a halt.

If you've ever worked out on a regular basis, then suddenly stopped for one reason or another, you know what this metabolic breakdown feels like. First it seems like you have less energy than you did before. Then your body starts to feel stiff and

unresponsive. Your digestion seems to be out of kilter and your hands and feet are always cold. You probably are more prone to depression and anxiety. Finally, the bathroom scale stops being your friend.

You return to your normal good health when you add regular exercise back into your life. This doesn't mean you need killer workouts to stay in shape. You can get by with forty-five minutes of aerobic and strengthening exercise three times a week. Better yet, add a few minutes of stretches every day and an additional exercise session or two each week. It could be something like shoveling snow vigorously or taking the dog on a long walk.

If you didn't develop the exercise habit as a child, take the time now to make exercise a regular part of your life. After just three weeks of regular workouts you will be hooked. Fitness experts say that we establish our lifetime patterns when we're in our twenties and thirties. It's never too late to start. Get the exercise habit today, and you'll enjoy better health and fitness for the rest of your life.

You will find that you feel better mentally and emotionally as well as physically. Mastering athletic skills, excelling at a chosen sport and developing a strong and capable body are all proven confidence-boosters. Studies show that the self-esteem of teenage

Yesterday I dared to struggle. Today I dare to **win.**

—Bernadette Devlin, Irish politician

Name That Muscle

Common terms you'll hear at the gym and in exercise classes

Abdominals (abs): Group of muscles across the abdomen.

Biceps: Muscle on the top of the upper arm, from the shoulder to the elbow. Popeye got a lot of mileage out of this one.

Gluteus (glutes): Three muscles that form the buttock. Gluteus maximus is the major fleshy one.

Hamstrings (hams): Pair of muscles on the back of the thigh.

Obliques: Abdominal muscles that start at the side of the waist and slant in and down at an angle toward the belly.

Quadriceps (quads): Large muscle on the front of the thigh that runs from the pelvis to the knee.

Triceps: Muscle that runs along the underside of the upper arm.

Warm-up: Starting a workout with easy exercises to slowly increase the heart and respiratory rate. This gets blood and oxygen to the muscles and "warms them up," thus reducing the risk of injury during the session.

Cool-down: Gradually reducing the intensity of the exercise at the end of a workout to slow the heart and respiratory rate.

Effortless Exercise

Researchers at Tufts University say that excess body fat is more likely the result of too much time in front of the TV than too much candy and cake. Getting enough exercise, they say, is the key to controlling weight.

You don't have to spend your whole life at the gym to stay in shape. Even moderately demanding exercise—carrying your baby around the house, mowing the lawn—adds to your daily workout. In fact, your daily activities burn off many more calories than your hour at the gym.

So what's the lesson? Boost the exercise you get throughout the day. Take the stairs instead of the elevator, walk to the corner store instead of driving or mulch the flower beds yourself. The goal is to get your metabolism up and running early in the morning and keep it going all day long.

girls noticeably increases when they participate in sports. Sports and other kinds of physical fitness activities teach us how to concentrate, set goals and respond to success and failure gracefully. Participation in sports can even be a vehicle for building new friendships.

Getting Started • If you're new to exercise or are out of practice, ease into it. Start by working out three times a week rather than every day so you don't burn out. If you're not sure how to perform an exercise, watch someone else or take a class and learn how to do it right. Be patient with yourself. Instant fitness won't come overnight.

Decide what you want to accomplish. Weight loss? A stronger upper body? Thinner thighs? Meet with a trainer to review your goals and put together a fitness plan. If you don't want to invest in the cost of a personal trainer, use the instructors at the gym. Aim for short- and long-term attainable goals.

Next, set aside specific times and days for exercise so you can get into a routine. This way you'll be less likely to skip a session or talk yourself out of a workout because you're feeling tired. But if you miss a session or two, don't punish yourself and use it as an excuse to stop altogether. Get right back into it and continue where you left off. If you go through a period where things are so hectic that you can't make it to the gym, don't stop, adapt. Take a brisk, thirty-minute walk at lunchtime. Buy an exercise video and a couple of five-pound weights, and do your workout at home.

Make it easy on yourself to get that needed exercise. Have the right clothing and equipment on hand to comfortably perform the activities you choose. Get enough sleep and nutrition so you have energy to support your body in exercise. Incorporate exercise into your social life, so it's not something you have to always do by yourself. Meet a friend for a class or a workout. Organize a skating party, a tennis game or a cross-country ski weekend. Join a soccer team or a hiking club.

Finally, review your progress every now and then. Take pride in your accomplishments, no matter how small. Graduated from a one-mile to a three-mile run? Mastered that difficult aerobics class? Able to stay on the stair machine for thirty minutes at a time now? Give yourself a pat on the back for your achievement. Recognize the goals you've reached, rather than dwelling on what you have left to attain.

Exercise Essentials • All workouts are not created equal. If you are rushing through the movements, flinging your arms around wildly or concentrating more on the magazine you're reading than on your muscles, you may not be getting all the benefits you could be.

• Stay in good form as you exercise. This means using your muscles rather than the momentum to do the movement. Remember to breathe and maintain good posture. Keep your joints fluid, rather than locking them in. Learn how you're supposed to move in the exercise, and do it correctly.

• Slow down and gain control. Think about the movement as you are doing it. If the aerobics teacher is moving too fast for you to keep up easily, modify the movement to do just the part of it that gives you the best workout. Rather than flinging a free weight up in the air, lift it slowly and correctly.

• Use resistance to help you increase the intensity of your workout. To get the most out of the movement, tense your muscles as you lift or push or stride. When lifting weights, work against gravity. Work your muscles during the return as well as on the lift.

• Extend your muscles as far as you can to use more of them in a movement. Reach far ahead with your arms when you're swimming freestyle. Stretch for the ball when playing tennis rather than letting a tough serve go unreturned. Take a yoga position as far as your body moves comfortably.

You can run hard, push, bite and sweat on the court and still be very much a woman.
—Sheryl Swoopes, All-American basketball player

Workout Choices •

Exercise doesn't have to be boring or deadly serious. There are a thousand ways to get your weekly quota of exercise. Mix and match activities to get the workout you want. Make it fun! Here are the most common activities to get your heart pumping, beginning with the best calorie-burning workouts.

Indoor Activities

Treadmill Running

Excellent lower-body workout. Adjust the incline and speed for your level of fitness.

Step Aerobics

Great for thighs and glutes. Shop around for a class or video where movements are not too complicated, so you get full aerobic benefits.

Climbing Stairs and Hills

Builds strength in legs, back and arms. Develops concentration and focus. Practitioners say it's even relaxing.

Stationary Bike

Exercises thighs while you catch up on your TV viewing. Vary the routine; saddle soreness and boredom get to some people.

Push-ups

Strengthens arms and chest like nothing else. Put aside those bad memories from gym class and give it another try.

Jump Rope

Excellent aerobic workout. Good for quads, calves, hamstrings and forearms.

Racquetball

Tightens arms, quads, shoulders, obliques and inner thighs. Reduces stress with every whack of the racquet.

Tai Chi

Tones the entire body. A relaxing, energizing exercise routine that you can practice into old age.

Treadmill Walking

Good lower-body workout. The steeper the incline, the better for the buttocks.

Ballet

Good overall conditioning and leg-toning. Who says you have to go to a sweaty gym to work out?

Judo, Karate, Tae Kwan Do

Builds coordination and strength. A good overall workout. Confidence grows when you learn how to defend yourself.

Weightlifting

Strengthens muscles. Free weights are best for the upper body, but use machines for the legs and glutes.

Swimming Laps

Sculpts legs, back and arms. Burns calories while being meditative. An exercise you can do for the rest of your life.

Aerobics

Great metabolism-booster and whole-leg workout. Shop around for a skillful instructor.

Stair Machine

Works the quads, hamstrings and glutes. Gets your heart rate going if you do it right.

Yoga
Tones the whole body. Relieves stress, improves breathing, stretches and relaxes muscles.

Cross-Country Ski Machine
Best full-body workout on a machine. Improves coordination.

Rowing Machine
Conditions the entire body. Unlike most other machines, gives the arms and shoulders a workout too.

Water Aerobics
Works the upper and lower body. A good choice for those with muscle soreness or problem joints.

Outdoor Activities

Running
Efficient lower-body workout. Burns fat and conditions legs, but hard on the knees and feet. Run on soft surfaces if you can.

Mountain Biking
Great for thighs and buttocks. Good cardiovascular workout if you keep up the speed and intensity.

Hiking
Offers the benefits of walking, but hills make it an even better workout.

Golf
Some conditioning, especially arms, shoulders and legs. Combines light exercise with socializing.

In-Line Skating
Tones those glutes. One of the fastest growing sports. Once you get proficient, it's great fun.

Backpacking
Good thigh, leg and buttock workout, especially on hills. Plus beautiful scenery, fresh air and a city escape.

Beach Volleyball
Good overall workout, especially with small teams. Playing on sand is great for toning legs.

Racewalking
All the benefits of walking, plus an upper-body workout. Sculpts legs.

Kayaking
Strengthens back, shoulders, obliques and arms. A soothing, peaceful sport.

Cross-Country Skiing
Best whole-body toner. Glide through inspiring mountain terrain while building muscles and stamina.

Tennis
Works forearms, quads, shoulders and obliques. Get a better workout with singles than with doubles tennis.

Walking
Slims quads, hamstrings, calves and glutes. The cardiovascular benefits of running, but at a more relaxed pace.

Shooting Baskets
Legs and arms get a workout. Benefits improve when playing on a full court.

Downhill Skiing
Works shoulders, back and legs. Not as good at fat-burning as cross-country skiing is, but still a workout. Plus it's exhilarating.

No-Equipment Workouts

• No time for the gym? Bad weather keeping you from your usual run? No need to interrupt your fitness routine—you can still get a rigorous workout at home. These exercises don't require any equipment.

Lunges are a great workout for your legs and buttocks. Because you're moving such large muscles, lunges get your heart and lungs pumping too. To do a lunge, stand erect with your feet together and your hands on your hips or at your side. Now take a big step forward with your left foot. Keeping your back straight, slowly bend your knees and lower your center of gravity to the ground. At the bottom of the move, your left thigh should be parallel to the ground and your left knee in line laterally with your left toes. When your right knee is just about to touch the floor and your right heel is off the ground, use your quadriceps (front of the thigh) to raise yourself, pressing your center of gravity up. Continue in sixty-second sets as long as you can in good form, then switch legs.

For a more intense workout, try walking lunges. Instead of pressing back up after lowering into a lunge, take a big step forward with your back leg. Continue in sixty-second sets for as long as you can in good form. Keep your back erect and go slow. Be sure to stretch the calves, thighs, buttocks and lower back when you are through.

Crunches are more effective, and better for your back, than the sit-ups you used to do in gym class. They are the best way to strengthen the abdominal muscles and get rid of a flabby middle. In the basic crunch, lie down with your lower back pressed to the floor or bench, your knees bent and your feet flat. Clasp your hands behind your neck lightly to support your head. Keep your elbows in and forward. Concentrate on your abdominals as you slowly lift your shoulders an inch or two off the floor or bench. This is the starting position. Now tighten your abs and slowly lift your shoulders a few inches higher while pressing your lower back to the ground. Hold this briefly, then slowly lower your shoulders to the starting position, giving your abs just as much attention as you did coming up. Concentrate on tensing your muscles to get more resistance, rather than going fast. Repeat. Do three sixty-second sets.

To work the oblique muscles, begin in the same starting position as the basic crunch. Pull your right leg up and rest the ankle on the left knee. Place your hands under your head, but with your elbows wide apart. Lift your left shoulder a few inches, keeping your right shoulder on the floor. Do three sixty-second sets of these, then switch legs and do the opposite side. Finish crunches with a stretch: Pull your knees up to your chest and relax.

Creating a Program •

To maintain or improve your fitness level, it's not enough to go out running four times a week, no matter how much distance you cover. A balanced exercise program is made up of three different types of activities: aerobic, strengthening and stretching. You don't need to get all three elements into one workout, but you should cover each one of them in the course of a week.

Aerobic exercise makes the heart beat faster and the breath come more rapidly. The blood carries oxygen to the muscles, which use it to burn calories. That's why when you're exercising, you want to be sure you are able to breathe comfortably. To strengthen the heart and lungs, exercise aerobically for twenty to thirty minutes, three times a week.

To build muscle strength and endurance, you have to move muscles against resistance. When you do muscle-strengthening exercises, you build bones as well, which is a big plus for women at risk for osteoporosis. Weightlifting is one of the best strengthening workouts, but pushups, crunches and pull-ups do the same thing. Perform thirty minutes of strengthening activity two to three times a week.

The final element in your exercise program should be stretching. Flexibility allows us to take muscles and joints through

Target Heart Rate

When you're exercising to burn fat, you want your heart to beat at a good pace during the aerobic portion of your workout—anywhere from 46 to 80 percent higher than it does when you're resting. (Unless you're in excellent

physical condition, aim for the lower percentage and you'll get more out of the workout.)

To figure your target heart rate, start with 220 and subtract your age. Then subtract your resting heart rate (the number of times it beats per minute when you are sitting still or just wake up). Multiply that by 46 percent (or higher), then add back your resting heart rate.

If you think you can, you can.

their full range of motion. This protects against injury and strain. Stretching exercises can be as simple as reaching toward the ceiling or making circles with the feet and ankles. Stretching can be a part of your workout, or done after you tumble out of bed in the morning. You need at least ten minutes of stretches a day, always preceded by a warm-up period.

Now that you know your weekly requirements, what should each of your exercise sessions look like? Start by warming up for five to ten minutes to get oxygen to the muscles. Do this by performing the exercise slowly, walking, jogging slowly or doing arm circles to get your blood going. You can also do some stretching after you've warmed up, but not before. (You risk tearing or pulling the muscles when they're cold.) Then it's time for the main exercise activity, which should last from twenty to forty-five minutes, depending on your endurance and fitness level. One day you might do a strengthening workout, another day an aerobic workout and other days a combination of the two. Then it's time to cool down (gradually slowing down your body's movements) and stretch for another five to ten minutes. Continue cooling down until your heartbeat returns to normal.

And if you think you can't, you're right.

—Mary Kay Ash, Cosmetics entrepreneur

Chapter 5

Staying Healthy

Good health is the foundation of true beauty. With health comes glowing skin, clear eyes, shiny hair and other physical attributes that no amount of makeup or clothing can replace. Health also brings vitality, energy and enthusiasm—personal qualities that illuminate our beauty and create a spark of excitement that is attractive to others.

Our bodies work so well that we take them for granted, not even thinking about the complex processes involved in keeping us alive. Each system of the body participates in an intricate ballet of interdependency: Our hearts circulate our blood, which is oxygenated

by our lungs, nourishing our muscles, enabling us to move and digest our food. Our health depends on the maintenance of this delicate balance.

We come in contact with infections and viruses continually, and most of the time we are able to fight them off. When we succumb to illnesses such as colds, flu, headaches and stomach upset, it is because something is out of balance in our lives, making us vulnerable. Illness and pain are a call to remedy that imbalance.

We can't change every factor that contributes to poor health—genetics are out of our control, and so is our environment sometimes. But we can do what we can to restore harmony in our lives by taking care of the basics—sleep, nutrition, exercise—and nurturing our minds and spirits as well. Health care should not begin when we get sick. Health care is what we do every day to strengthen our bodies' own defenses against illness and maintain our natural state of good health.

Changing Bad Habits

• Just because you've been doing something one way for a long time doesn't mean you have to do it the same way forever. Everything you do is a choice. A behavior that once worked for you may no longer seem appropriate or necessary. It may be time for a change.

Start by thinking about what needs you are satisfying with a bad habit. If you want to give up smoking, first think about what (besides the nicotine addiction) prompts you to smoke. Every time you feel an urge for a cigarette, think about the circumstances that triggered the impulse. Perhaps you get nervous at parties and like to have something to do with your hands. Maybe you smoke when you need to take a break from your work. Once you know what need smoking fulfills in you, you can find another way to satisfy that need. You can munch on carrot sticks instead of smoking a cigarette or take a short walk when you need a work break. You can eliminate the need entirely through therapy, hypnosis or some other program. Sometimes we just outgrow our unhealthy needs naturally.

Give yourself plenty of time to make a change. Don't set yourself up to fail by expecting achievements that you would never expect from anyone else. If you've been doing something one way for ten years, you will take more than a day to learn to do it differently.

Most lasting changes take time. Even if you quit smoking overnight, you may take a few months or even years before you feel entirely free of the temptation.

Change can be difficult, so give yourself a lot of support and credit for trying. Look at mistakes or slip-ups as the learning experiences that they are, rather than as signs of your weakness. If you're feeling stressed out, think about what nice thing you can do for yourself to make it easier. Seek out support from other people.

Express Yourself • Singing the blues when you're feeling down is not only good for the soul, it's good for your health as well.

Medical researchers are finding that there is a close relationship between our emotions and our physical health. When we release emotions, our immune systems produce extra T-cells (a type of white blood cells), which protect us by fighting off infections.

It is better to acknowledge and release any emotion, including sadness, than it is to feel nothing at all. After all, when we are depressed is when we are most at risk for illness. Suppressing our emotions appears to suppress our immune system as well. At least one study has linked increased rates of breast cancer to suppressed feelings of anger and grief.

If you want to stay healthy, get rid of that stiff upper lip and have a good cry or a hearty laugh instead.

Fear less, hope more,
eat less, chew more,
whine less, breathe more,
talk less, say more,
hate less, love more
and all good things
will be yours.

—Swedish Proverb

Body Awareness Exercise

Our bodies are sensitive instruments that let us know right away how we are feeling. When we are in an uncomfortable situation, our muscles tighten, our digestion goes awry, and our breathing gets more shallow. When our resistance to illness is down, our bodies feel fatigued and achy before we actually get sick. By learning to read these signals from our bodies, we can avoid or alter stressful situations and head off illness before it sets in.

This exercise will help you become more aware of the state of your health. You can do it while sitting at work, standing in the grocery line or lying in bed. Answer the questions by taking a problem-solving approach.

How does your body feel overall? Are your muscles tense or relaxed? Is there soreness anywhere? Do you feel energetic or tired?______________________________

____

Listen to your breath. Are you breathing deeply or shallowly? Does your breath come easily? Does your chest feel relaxed or tight?______________________________

____

How is your posture? Are your shoulders back and your spine straight, or are you slumped over? Is there tension in your neck and shoulders? How about in your jaw and temples? Do your eyes feel any strain? Are your arms and hands relaxed and comfortable?______________________________

____

Do you have any pain or strain in your lower back? Are the muscles in your buttocks and legs relaxed? Is there any soreness in your knees or feet? ______________________________

____

What about your abdomen? Is there any tension there? Are you experiencing any problems with your digestion?______________________________

____

If you find your body is tense or not at ease, think about what might be causing the discomfort. If you are feeling healthy and vital, think about what conditions are making that possible. ___________

____

If you are feeling any stress or tension, would taking care of a physical need such as sleep, food or exercise help? ___________

____

Have you experienced a stressful situation lately? If the answer is yes, what can you do to make yourself feel better right now? Do you need to raise a difficult issue with someone or make a change?

____

____

- Put the situation in perspective: Think of three ways you could have handled it worse and three ways you could have handled it better. ___________

  ____

  ____

  ____

- If you can't control the source of the stress, is there anything you can do to change your response to it? ___________

  ____

  ____

  ____

What is the kindest thing you can do for yourself and your body today? ___________

____

Now how does your body feel? ___________

____

____

Minimize Toxins • Toxic chemicals can place a great stress on our bodies and even make us sick. Reactions can range from mild breathing difficulties, skin rashes and headaches, to a total breakdown of the immune system. It's almost impossible to escape exposure to toxins completely, as they have become integral to modern life. But you can limit your intake of them and take steps to help your body rid itself of those you have consumed.

Food and water are two areas where you have some choices in what you consume. Drink water rather than soft drinks. Buy purified or spring water or filter it yourself. Buy as much chemical-free food as possible. Today you can find not only organic fruits and vegetables, but also organic dairy products, prepared foods and grains in the supermarket. Avoid tobacco smoke and minimize your consumption of drugs. Keep dangerous chemicals out of the home. Use natural cleansers such as baking soda and borax, which are just as effective as chemical cleaning products.

You can help your body shed toxins by drinking more water and eating more fiber. You can sweat out toxins through regular aerobic exercise and by sitting in saunas, steam rooms or whirlpools. You can neutralize the toxins by taking antioxidant vitamins and minerals. Many herbs are helpful at speeding up the elimination of toxins and in cleansing organs that process them. For example, milk thistle extract has been shown to aid the liver. Kelp (seaweed) neutralizes radiation exposure.

Health is beauty, and the most perfect health is the most perfect beauty.
—William Shenstone, Writer

Natural Healers • Herbal medicine, practiced worldwide for thousands of years, is a gentle way of building up the body's immunity, easing symptoms and treating illness.

The Chinese were said to have discovered the medicinal value of herbs around 3400 B.C. A Chinese herbal classic written about that time listed 237 herbal prescriptions using dozens of herbs, including ephedra, which is used today in decongestants. Traditional Chinese medicine still relies heavily on herbal therapy. Ayurvedic medicine, the world's oldest healing practice, used herbs such as ginger, cinnamon and senna. Egyptian herbal healers were considered the finest healers in the

Mediterranean and introduced herbal healing to Europe. They believed garlic and onion strengthened the body and prevented disease. Benedictine monks were avid herbalists who borrowed the Arab practice of flavoring wine with digestion-promoting herbs, creating the forerunner of today's liqueurs. A woman folk-healer introduced a British physician to foxglove, which contains the heart-drug digitalis. American Indians used herbs extensively and taught white settlers about the many healing herbs on American soil, including echinacea, goldenseal, sarsaparilla and witch hazel.

Many prescription and over-the-counter medications, such as aspirin, were at one time plant-based. The use of herbs in the United States diminished when drugs became available. Today herbal healing is experiencing a resurgence of popularity.

Herbs support the body's ability to heal itself by cleansing and strengthening the tissues. They are natural antibiotics, antivirals, antifungals, antiseptics, diuretics and sedatives. Although herbs should be used with caution and moderation, they are typically much easier on the body and safer than prescription drugs. They are also a lot less expensive. At least sixteen herbs have been approved by the FDA to be safe and effective, allowing them to carry health claims. These include slippery elm bark (for sore throat) and psyllium seeds (a laxative), which are sold under various brand names.

There are different ways to ingest herbs. *Infusions* are extracts made from herbs with medicinal qualities in their flowers, stems and leaves. An infusion typically calls for one-half to one ounce of a dried herb (double the amount for fresh) to soak in a pint of boiling water for ten to twenty minutes. *Decoctions* are prepared like infusions except they are made from roots and bark. *Tinctures* are concentrated extracts of herbs made with alcohol or glycerin rather than water. Less than twenty drops is needed for a typical dose. Dried herbs come in capsule form. Some herbs are made into poultices (moist paste) and salves (ointment) and applied topically.

When using herbs, always use only the recommended amounts for recommended periods, and pay attention to symptoms of toxicity or allergy. Be careful with herbal weight-loss preparations, which may increase the heart and breath rates and act as diuretics, depleting the body of potassium. Consult a physician before taking medicinal herbs if you're taking other drugs or if you're pregnant or nursing, and do not give herbs to children under two without consulting a pediatrician.

Herbs and Their Healing Properties

Herb	Conditions It May Aid
Aloe	wounds, burns, scalds, infections
Anise Seed	indigestion, gas, bad breath, cough, bronchitis, asthma
Arnica Flower	bruises, sprains, strains
Balm Leaves (lemon balm, bee balm, melissa, sweet balm)	wounds, genital herpes, cold sores, fever, digestion problems, gas, muscle tension, anxiety

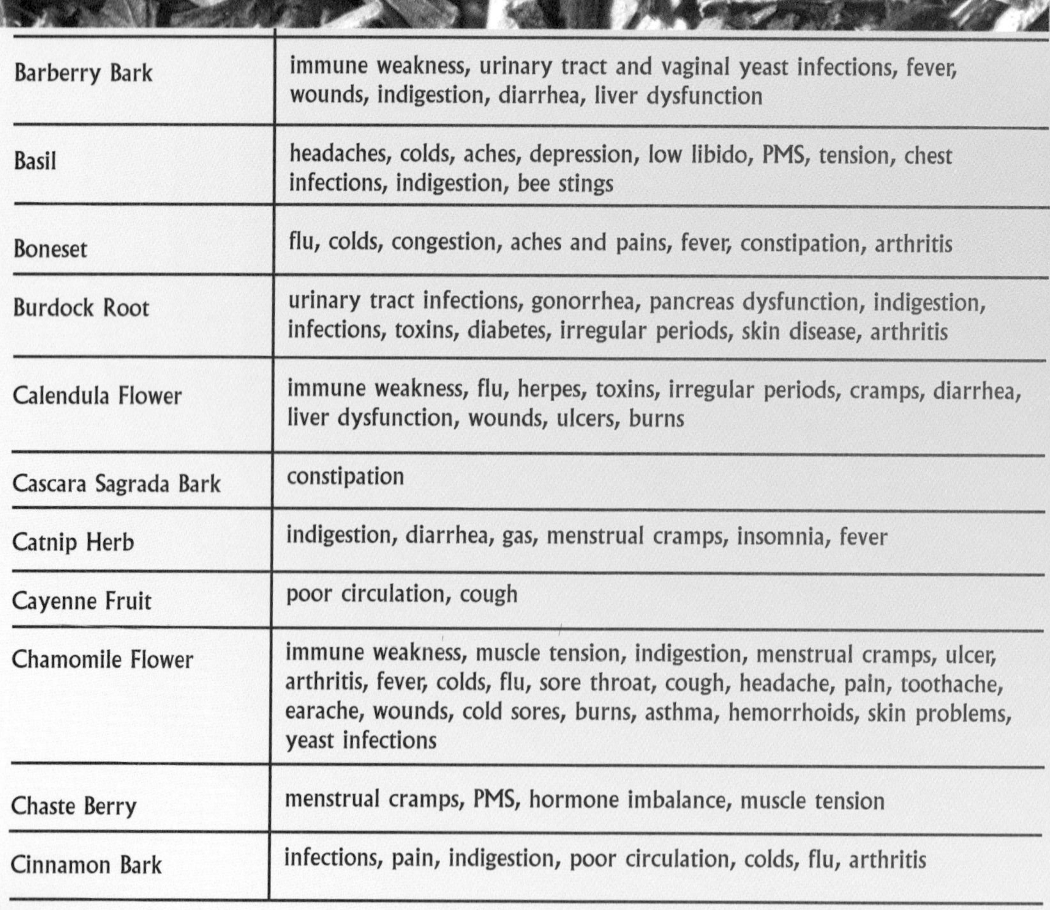

Herb	Conditions It May Aid
Barberry Bark	immune weakness, urinary tract and vaginal yeast infections, fever, wounds, indigestion, diarrhea, liver dysfunction
Basil	headaches, colds, aches, depression, low libido, PMS, tension, chest infections, indigestion, bee stings
Boneset	flu, colds, congestion, aches and pains, fever, constipation, arthritis
Burdock Root	urinary tract infections, gonorrhea, pancreas dysfunction, indigestion, infections, toxins, diabetes, irregular periods, skin disease, arthritis
Calendula Flower	immune weakness, flu, herpes, toxins, irregular periods, cramps, diarrhea, liver dysfunction, wounds, ulcers, burns
Cascara Sagrada Bark	constipation
Catnip Herb	indigestion, diarrhea, gas, menstrual cramps, insomnia, fever
Cayenne Fruit	poor circulation, cough
Chamomile Flower	immune weakness, muscle tension, indigestion, menstrual cramps, ulcer, arthritis, fever, colds, flu, sore throat, cough, headache, pain, toothache, earache, wounds, cold sores, burns, asthma, hemorrhoids, skin problems, yeast infections
Chaste Berry	menstrual cramps, PMS, hormone imbalance, muscle tension
Cinnamon Bark	infections, pain, indigestion, poor circulation, colds, flu, arthritis

Herb	Conditions It May Aid
Clove	toothache, gum problems, indigestion, infections, diarrhea
Corn Silk	water retention, kidney and bladder trouble
Cramp-bark	muscle tension and spasms, painful periods, cramps
Cranberry	water retention, kidney, bladder and urinary tract infections
Dandelion Root/Leaf	water retention, constipation, high cholesterol, high blood pressure, yeast infection, gallstones, toxins, indigestion, skin problems, headache, potassium and vitamin A and C deficiency
Dill Seed	indigestion, gas, urinary tract infection, bad breath, diarrhea
Dong Quai Root	female hormone imbalance, menstrual cramps, PMS, anxiety
Echinacea Root	immune weakness, sore throat, flu, colds, infections, allergies, wounds, infectious disease, tonsillitis, bronchitis, tuberculosis, urinary tract and yeast infections, wounds, arthritis, tumors, blood toxins, eczema, fatigue, poor circulation
Eucalyptus	colds, flu, phlegm, cuts
Fennel Seed	indigestion, gas, obesity
Feverfew Leaf/Flower	rheumatoid arthritis, headache, migraine, asthma, bronchitis, insect bites, high blood pressure, indigestion, fever, PMS, menstrual cramps, sciatica and other nerve pain, hay fever, dizziness, tinnitus
Flax Seed	constipation
Garlic Bulb/Seed	colds, flu, bronchitis, infections, high blood pressure and cholesterol, heart disease and stroke, high blood sugar, sore throat, indigestion, gas, hay fever, sinusitis, fever, cramps, cancer prevention
Ginger Root	motion sickness, nausea, indigestion, gas, menstrual cramps, colds, flu, immunity weakness, arthritis, fever, reduced appetite, high blood pressure and cholesterol, poor circulation

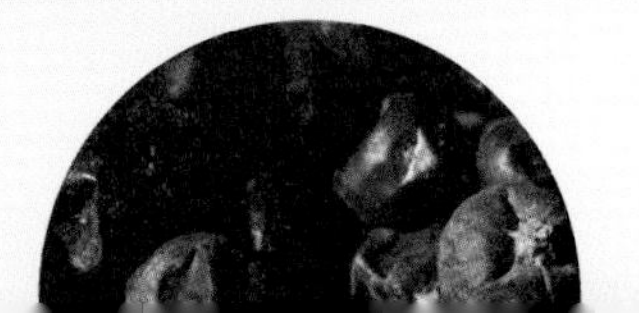

Herb	Conditions It May Aid
Ginkgo Biloba	poor memory, strokes, tinnitus, dizziness, asthma, headache, depression
Ginseng Root	stress, poor memory, anxiety, depression, high blood pressure, indigestion, disease resistance, fatigue, reduced physical stamina, immune weakness, high cholesterol, diabetes, radiation therapy, insomnia
Hops	anxiety, tension, insomnia, indigestion
Horehound Herb	congestion
Hyssop Leaf	insomnia, congestion, cough, herpes, cold sores
Licorice Root	constipation, cough, respiratory congestion, ulcers, arthritis, infections, hepatitis, cirrhosis, heartburn, indigestion, high cholesterol, cough, headache, fever, stress
Marjoram	indigestion, herpes, menstrual cramps
Meadowsweet	indigestion, heartburn, nausea, gastritis, ulcers, fever, headache, arthritis, menstrual cramps, inflammation, diarrhea, hernia, gas, water retention
Milk Thistle Seed	liver toxicity
Myrrh Gum	mouth sores, sore throat, gingivitis, sinusitis, cavity-making bacteria, cuts, abrasions

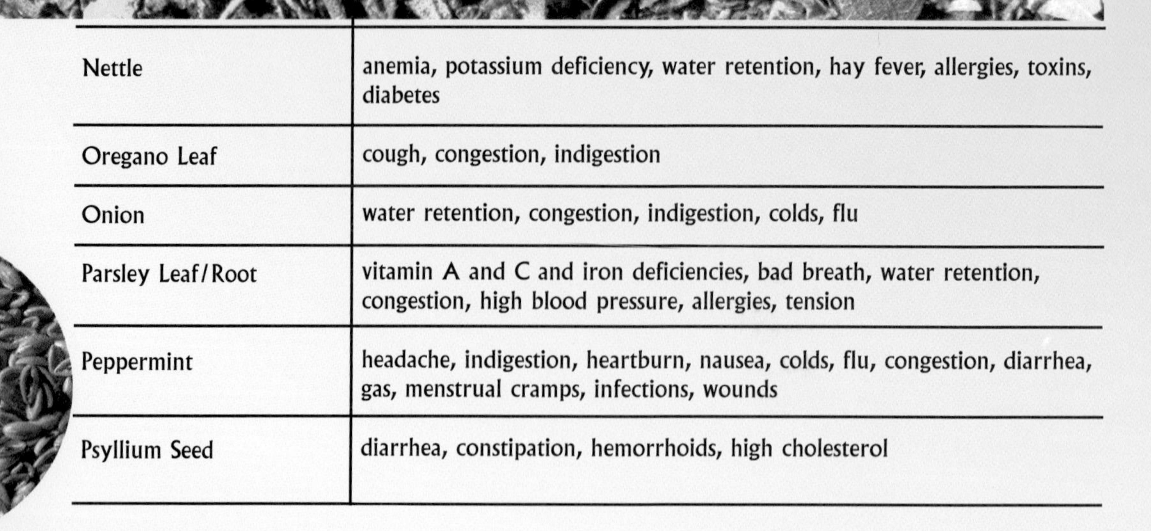

Herb	Conditions It May Aid
Nettle	anemia, potassium deficiency, water retention, hay fever, allergies, toxins, diabetes
Oregano Leaf	cough, congestion, indigestion
Onion	water retention, congestion, indigestion, colds, flu
Parsley Leaf/Root	vitamin A and C and iron deficiencies, bad breath, water retention, congestion, high blood pressure, allergies, tension
Peppermint	headache, indigestion, heartburn, nausea, colds, flu, congestion, diarrhea, gas, menstrual cramps, infections, wounds
Psyllium Seed	diarrhea, constipation, hemorrhoids, high cholesterol

Herb	Conditions It May Aid
Red Clover	blood toxins
Red Pepper	indigestion, diarrhea, chronic pain, cluster headaches
Rose Hips	vitamin C deficiency, water retention, colds, flu, exhaustion, constipation
Rosemary Leaf	immune weakness, tension headache, depression, muscular pain, neuralgia, sciatica, colds, sinus congestion, bacteria, fever, respiratory illness, poor circulation, anxiety, tension, exhaustion, indigestion, gas
Sage	constipation, indigestion, wounds, sore throat, canker sores
St. John's Wort	bruises, strains, sprains, burns, wounds, congestion, depression, viral infections
Saw Palmetto	prostate enlargement and infection, female infertility, painful periods, urinary tract infection, tension, anxiety
Slippery Elm	sore throat, diarrhea, burns, cuts, wounds, cough, ulcers, irritable bladder, cystitis, indigestion
Thyme Leaf and Flower	laryngitis, tonsillitis, sore throat, cough, fever, worms, indigestion, menstrual cramps
Valerian Root	tension, anxiety, insomnia, intestinal colic, menstrual cramps, migraine, rheumatic pain, high blood pressure
Vervain	insomnia, muscle tension, depression, headache, migraine, liver, fever, mouth sores
White Willow Bark	headache, neuralgia, fever, hay fever, arthritis, rheumatism, muscle pain, inflammation, menstrual cramps
Witch Hazel	hemorrhoids, scalds, burns, swelling, bleeding
Yarrow Flower	flu, fever, colds, toxin buildup, high blood pressure, pain, indigestion, menstrual cramps, wounds, insomnia, tension
Yellow Dock Root	anemia, hepatitis, chronic skin disorders, constipation, indigestion

Checkups to Get

Regular medical exams should become part of your health care program. Make time in your life for the following checkups that are particularly important for women.

Pap Smear and Pelvic Exam

Annually. Schedule gynecological exams twice a year if you've had an irregular Pap smear, or have genital warts or herpes. After 40, you may want to get a mammogram regularly.

General Physical

Visit your general practitioner or internist every one to five years, depending on what you and your doctor think is appropriate. After age 50, visit once every two years.

Dental Exam

Get a checkup once a year and teeth cleaned every six months to a year.

Breasts Self-Exam

Check your breasts for lumps or irregularities every month, three to four days after the end of your period.

Skin Self-Exam

Once a month check your whole body for new or changing moles. If you notice any, visit a dermatologist right away.

Ailments & Remedies • Many common ailments can be treated through preventive care, diet, herbs and exercise without using potentially harmful drugs. Here are some remedies to consider:

Colds and Flu: You can often ward off a cold or flu—or at least minimize their symptoms—if you take good care of yourself when the illness is just coming on.

Getting extra rest when you're feeling run down is the best thing you can do to help your body fight off colds and flu. When symptoms such as headache, achiness and sneezing start to appear, immediately begin taking one or all of the following to strengthen your immune system: vitamin C (500-milligram tablet a few times a day), garlic (fresh cloves or in odor-free capsules) and echinacea extract (20 drops three times a day). Drink plenty of water to help eliminate toxins and replace fluids lost from a fever.

Sip mint, chamomile, thyme, ginger or sage tea to clear your sinuses, soothe a headache, break a fever and relax your muscles. Other herbs that have been known to benefit cold and flu are boneset, slippery elm, ginseng root, St. John's wort, Oregon grape root and horehound. Gargling with salt water will help reduce inflammation and pain, and also clear secretions. Licorice lozenges are a natural expectorant, as are honey and tea and hot lemonade.

Eat lightly (clear broths and diluted fruit juice) so your body can concentrate on fighting the infection. Chicken soup is touted as a good food to help fight a cold, and there's real merit to this claim. The onion and garlic used to season the soup, along with a substance released from the chicken, fight bacteria and viruses and also boost immunity. For extra help, add some ginger root to the broth—it's good for fever, it's an expectorant and it strengthens the body's immune system. Put in plenty of pepper and spices too—they will stimulate the glands in your nose to release secretions that fight infection.

A massage, hot bath or heating pad may feel good. Breathe moist air from a shower or steam vaporizer to clear your head. Open a window for some fresh air if the weather is not too cold.

Headaches: Start by figuring out what caused your headache so you can find the proper remedy. Tension headaches are common and can be caused by eyestrain, stress, lack of sleep or bad nutrition. Try a relaxation exercise called "palming." First, rub your hands together vigorously to warm them. Then close your eyes and cover them with your hands so that your palms are over your eyes and your fingers are on your forehead, extending up to your scalp. Cup them a little, shutting out the light. Do some deep breathing, meditation or guided imagery, taking yourself to a peaceful place in your mind. Do this for five to twenty minutes. You can also try dabbing rosemary oil on your forehead, temple and behind your ears, or putting a vinegar-soaked compress on your forehead.

Other alternative headache remedies include ice or heat on the forehead or back of the neck, a warm bath, biofeedback, stretches and acupressure. To do your own acupressure, squeeze the web between your forefinger and

Mood Boosters

Exercising is the best way to beat a bad mood, according to a California State University psychology study. Listening to music also can help send a bad mood packing. Other ways to pick yourself up include socializing, adjusting your thoughts and engaging in a religious or spiritual activity.

thumb, or press the points on either side of your spine at the base of your neck.

Your headache may be caused by low blood sugar, which is solved by eating a nutritious snack or meal. Is it a sinus headache? Massage the area over your sinus cavities, and inhale the aromatic steam from some hot peppermint, sage or rosemary tea. If it's due to bad air—smog, toxins, smoke—get some fresh air immediately. Allergies can also cause headaches. Pay attention to what foods or other allergens precede your headaches, and eliminate those from your life if you can. A headache from a hangover can be helped by drinking fruit juice with a pinch of salt to replace lost nutrients. If you've missed your daily dose of coffee, your headache may be caused by caffeine withdrawal.

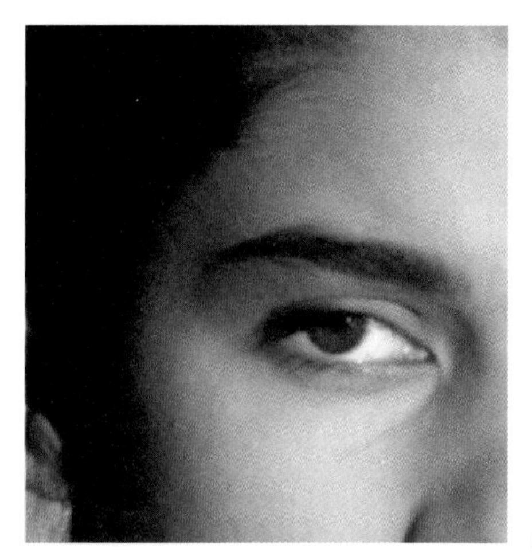

Migraines are hard to stop once they take hold. To help prevent their onset, take steps to release tension that builds up in your shoulders and neck. Take plenty of gentle exercise every day. Eat a healthy diet free of coffee, fried foods and refined sugar.

Consult your doctor immediately if the headache is different than those you usually get, particularly if it's sudden and severe, gets progressively worse and arrives after a blow to the head, a recent sore throat or an ear or respiratory infection. Also check with the doctor if your headache is accompanied by a stiff neck, persistent fever, vomiting or convulsions; if it gets worse after coughing, straining or sudden movement; or if you're also experiencing neurological symptoms such as speech or vision problems, numbness, confusion or loss of consciousness.

It is part of the cure to want to be cured.

—Seneca, Philosopher

Premenstrual Syndrome: PMS describes the cluster of recurring symptoms that some women experience up to a week or two before their menstrual periods and one day into their periods. Physical symptoms can include headaches, migraines, joint and muscle aches and swelling, backaches, food cravings, thirst, decreased alcohol tolerance, constipation, diarrhea, sweating, bloating, weight gain, breast tenderness, clumsiness, changes in sex drive, acne and allergies. Psychological symptoms might include loss of emotional control, depression, mood swings, anxiety, forgetfulness, decreased concentration, nightmares, hostility and loss of self-confidence.

Diet can play a big role in decreasing the intensity of PMS suffering. Eat smaller but more frequent meals before your period. Consume plenty of complex carbohydrates—especially whole grains and leafy greens—to keep your energy and mood levels up. Raw and dried fruits, nuts, seeds and cold-pressed oils are also excellent, and calcium-rich foods such as yogurt help as well. Take a multivitamin supplement to supply any nutrients you may be missing. Avoid refined sugars, which can cause depression, and keep caffeine to a minimum because it can increase your anxiety, irritability and muscle tension. Alcohol can make headaches, fatigue and depression worse. Lighten up on the salt.

Exercise can ease cramps and improve your mood. Satisfying sex can also help reduce the pain of cramps. Acupuncture has been reported to reduce abdominal cramps.

You may need more sleep right before your period and feel less alert overall. Give yourself an extra hour or two of sleep at night if you need it or take a nap when you feel run down. Don't over-schedule yourself; take it easy during this time.

Be sure to get enough calcium, magnesium, Vitamin A, vitamin B6 and Vitamin E, either through diet or in supplements. (PMS vitamin formulas are available at most supermarkets and drugstores.) Natural diuretics, such as parsley, dandelion leaf and nettle teas and watermelon, can minimize bloating. Herbs such as cramp-bark, black cohash root, valerian root, dong quai root, chaste berry, blue vervain, oat seed, passionflower and evening primrose oil can help with cramps, tension and mood swings.

Digestion Problems: Constipation, diarrhea, nausea and gas are the result of incomplete or disrupted digestion. They can be caused by such behaviors as eating too quickly, not chewing food well enough, overeating, smoking, eating the wrong food combinations, maintaining the wrong diet, eating too much sugar or salt and eating when upset.

Create a calming atmosphere during your meals and try not to eat on the run. Eat a balanced diet and pay attention to what foods don't agree with you; food allergies are a fairly common problem. In general, eat a diet of whole fresh foods, whole grains, green and yellow vegetables, juices and yogurt.

Naturally fibrous foods, such as fresh vegetables, whole grains, oat bran and prunes, can relieve constipation. Helpful herbs include alfalfa leaf, apple pectin, buckthorn bark, cascara sagrada, dandelion root, flax and psyllium seed. Drink plenty of liquids and increase the amount of exercise you get.

To reduce problems with gas, eat protein-rich foods early in the meal—*before* salads and vegetables—and not after the meal. Do not mix too many different foods at the same meal, especially proteins and fruits and starches. Always include green leafy vegetables with proteins. Drink a glass of warm water with the juice of half a lemon added to aid digestion. Eat slowly and try to avoid eating when you're upset. Helpful herbs include dandelion, chamomile, cardamon seeds and goldenseal tea. A number of products now on the market help eliminate gas too.

When bothered by diarrhea, avoid milk products except for yogurt. Try a potassium- and sodium-rich sports drink or drink bouillon and fruit juice with a little salt added to replace lost nutrients. Drink plenty of liquids to replace those that were lost. Herbal teas that contain chamomile, cinnamon and ginger can help.

Pamper Yourself •

Sometimes it seems easier to take care of our responsibilities to other people than it is to take care of ourselves. It takes effort to get enough sleep each night, prepare and eat nutritious meals, and honor our bodies with adequate exercise. But as the saying goes, an ounce of prevention is worth a pound of cure.

Taking a *mental health* day now and then can be another preventive measure. If you're feeling a little achy or tired, why not cancel that obligation that's really not so important, and go to bed early? Ask someone else to do the shopping and cook dinner. Or take a day off to stay home and relax with a couple of videos, read a novel or just sleep. Taking a day now might save you from a week in bed with the flu when you can least afford it.

As well as these important healthful activities, there are a variety of other pleasing activities that add to your well-being. Treat yourself to a spa vacation in the privacy of your own home. Enjoy calming herbal baths, energizing body scrubs and soothing scented massages. Meditation and breathing exercises will help you tap your inner resources in a new way. Learning to give yourself pleasure breaks is another way to cultivate beauty.

A merry heart doeth good like a medicine.

—Proverbs 17:22

Chapter 6

Scent & Aromatherapy

Our natural scents are like our fingerprints. They are unique to each of us—our personal signatures. Each of our smells is so distinctive that children and their mothers can identify each other by scent alone. Even perfume cannot change that. Fragrance reacts to each person's body chemistry differently, creating a unique scent for each wearer.

Smell was our first and most powerful sense. In the early stages of our evolutionary development, we used it to find a mate and detect danger. Though other senses have gained in dominance, we still rely heavily on our sense of smell. Scent often registers

on a subliminal level, though sometimes it becomes conscious. We are attracted to someone because we like the way he smells. We also say that we can smell fear on someone or we "smell danger in the air."

The perfume we wear should make us feel good and match the occasion and the season. Fragrance creates a mood and tells others something about us. Are you a romantic who loves feminine, floral fragrances? Or do you like the complexity of an oriental blend, or the clean crispness of a citrus scent? Spicy, woodsy fragrances go well with cold weather, when they are appropriately stimulating and energetic. In hot weather, lighter floral, grassy and citrus fragrances are typically refreshing and light.

Whatever the fragrance, it should be applied with a light touch. A fragrance is most pleasing when it is a soft whisper that makes others want to come closer, rather than a shout that keeps them away.

Scent Strengths

Type	% of Fragrance Essence
Perfume	15% to 30%
Eau de Parfum	8% to 15%
Eau de Toilette	4% to 8%
Eau de Cologne	2% to 5%
Splash Cologne	1% to 3%

Scents and Sensibilities •

Throughout history, men and women have adorned their bodies, hair, clothes and rooms with flower and herb essences. In early Mesopotamia incense was burned as a fragrant offering to the gods. Egyptians, six thousand years ago, used plant essences extensively for cosmetic purposes, healing and embalming their dead. In the Bible, the three kings were said to have presented the Christ child with frankincense and myrrh. The Greeks and Romans were known to soak in scented baths and wear perfume. In the seventeenth century, the French town of Grasse became a center for perfumery and remains so today.

In the eighteenth and nineteenth centuries, lavender, violet and rose were favorite scents. In the twentieth century, new multi-floral and spicy oriental blends were created, and synthetics, known as aldehydes, made any scent possible. As with fashions in clothing, fragrance preferences change from decade to decade. The sexual revolution of the sixties and seventies was accompanied by musk and patchouli. In the power-dressing eighties, heady oriental scents carried the day. In the nineties, popular perfumes feature fresh, light, natural, fruity and herbal scents.

Anatomy of a Perfume • The typical perfume is not merely a blend of essential oils. It is a complex layering of three fragrance groupings, called *notes,* which wash over us in waves.

The top note or head note is the first impression of the scent on the skin. The fragrance lasts less than a minute, for it is comprised of light scent molecules such as citrus, delicate florals, grasses and aldehydes, which evaporate quickly. The top note carries the energy of the scent that hooks you right away. Then as the fragrance interacts with skin chemistry it produces the heart note or middle note, which contains the rich floral scents. The base note, which emerges later, is considered the true personality of the perfume. It blends with your own personal scent and lingers for several hours. Warm woods and animal scents such as sandalwood, vanilla, musk and cedar are accompanied by fixatives, which give them staying power.

Fragrance Families • Buying just the right perfume for you can be a lengthy process. Perfumes do not carry ingredient lists that tell you what you are getting, nor are they arranged by type. Instead, your nose has to do the shopping. That often means wading into the perfume section and trying on a multitude

Scent & the Brain

When we inhale a fragrance, it travels back into the nasal cavity where it is dissolved in the mucus of five million cells that connect to the olfactory area of the brain via long nerve fibers. When the brain's smell center detects a scent, it sends a message to the limbic system, which controls emotion, memory, sex drive and intuition. The information also goes to the hypothalamus, which controls the body's neurochemicals and hormones.

As a survival mechanism, the brain responds immediately to

a smell to determine whether it is pleasurable or not and whether or not it is a threat. Smell is so intertwined with memory and emotion that we can smell a fragrance worn by a former beau years later and immediately feel fondness, pain or nostalgia. A smell can transport us back to another time in our lives like no other sense.

Common Scents

Floral fragrances are what we like to wear most often, according to a *Self* magazine survey. Thirty-four percent of

the magazine's readers chose florals as their favorite perfume, while a quarter of those surveyed liked fruity and citrus scents best. Musky, spicy and natural scents each attracted a little more than 10 percent of perfume wearers. Herbal and woodsy scents drew 5 and 3 percent respectively.

of scents with nothing but the name and bottle design to guide you in making a selection.

But there is a rhyme and reason to perfume design. Fragrances are divided into five families—floral, oriental, woodsy/mossy, citrus and green. Within these families are subtypes, which are created by blending elements of other groups.

Florals make up the largest family of fragrances. Some of the most popular flowers for perfume are jasmine, ylang-ylang, hyacinth, honeysuckle, tuberose, lilac, lily of the valley, narcissus, rose, gardenia, violet, carnation, lavender, orange blossom and magnolia. Some floral fragrances are based on a single variety of flower, such as gardenia or rose, but most are blends of several types of flowers. Floral scents are typically blended with other types of fragrances for complexity. There are green florals with herbs, leaves and grasses; fruity florals with peaches, apples and berries; light florals, which are blended with citrus; aldehyde florals with synthetic fragrances; amber florals, which are mixed with vanilla, balsam and spice; and oriental florals, which are made of exotic flowers and spice, balsam or resin.

Oriental fragrances have a mysterious, full-bodied scent and are made of spices, musk, resins, exotic flowers and balsam. These are the heaviest fragrances and are often used for cool weather and evenings. Two varieties are oriental amber, one of which blends citrus with amber and vanilla. The other is oriental spice, which adds elements of cinnamon, nutmeg, vanilla, pepper, clove, ginger, coriander and cardamom, as well as spicy florals such as carnation and lavender, and musk and wood scents.

The third category of fragrance is woodsy/mossy. These scents combine fresh citrus with earthy oakmoss and sometimes patchouli. They are natural, soft, sweet and warm scents. In the fruity variation, peach is added for a heavy scent. Citrus is the

Today a new sun rises for me; everything lives, everything is animated...

dominant element in a lighter type. Sometimes florals such as rose and gardenia are added to the woodsy/mossy base. Another variation adds floral and musk or ambergris notes for a full, warm scent. A sporty green fragrance is created with the addition of grasses, leaves and herbs, as well as conifer notes such as pine and juniper.

Refreshing, casual citrus fragrances may contain lemon, bergamot, tangerine and lime. Variations are created with the addition of floral, green and woodsy notes.

The last category is the green family, crisp, sporty scents that incorporate sage, rosemary, pine, juniper, grasses, leaves, lavender, chamomile, hyacinth and basil. The herbs, grasses and leaves in these fragrances are often blended with florals and musky scents for complexity.

Therapeutic Scent • What if someone told you she had something that would help you feel more alert, improve your memory, relax your tense muscles and help you sleep—just for starters? What if she added that this miracle potion had no side effects, was available without a prescription and was relatively inexpensive. Would you be interested?

These are just some of the benefits attributed to aromatherapy, the therapeutic use of natural distilled, essential oils from the fruit, seeds, flowers, roots, leaves, resin, bark and wood of plants. Like herbal medicine, aromatherapy works by strengthening the body's own healing mechanisms, making it safer to use than most drugs.

The antiseptic and antibiotic powers of herbal preparations were documented in France in the 1920s, which is where the term

everything invites me to cherish it.

—Anne De Lenclos, 17th-century courtesan

aromatherapy was born. Its expansion in Europe can be attributed to the publication of *Aromatherapie: The Treatment of Illness with the Essence of Place* by Dr. Jean Valnet, who used herbal medicine to effectively treat French soldiers' wounds during World War II. Today aromatherapy is widely practiced in Europe. In France it is recognized as a medical specialty and covered by national health insurance.

Aromatherapy can be used to alter mood and neutralize stress. Scientists have shown that beta brain waves, which produce a state of heightened awareness, are increased when stimulating oils, such as peppermint, rosemary or basil, are inhaled. Calming oils, such as neroli, jasmine, lavender and rose, produce more alpha and theta brain waves, which create relaxation and a sense of well-being. Patients who were exposed to a vanilla scent while undergoing medical tests were less anxious, in a Memorial Sloan-Kettering Cancer Center study. In a Japanese study of keypunch operators and aromatherapy, lemon scent was effective at reducing errors by 54 percent, jasmine by 33 percent and lavender by 21 percent. Lily of the valley and peppermint fragrance had similar effects in another study of computer workers.

Practicing Aromatherapy • You can find essential oils in skin and bath care stores, department stores, health food stores, at spas and through the mail. The price of an essential oil varies, depending on the availability and cost of the plant it is derived from and the quantity it takes to make an

Smell is the sense of the imagination.
—Jean Jacques Rousseau, Philosopher

Aromatherapy Massage Recipes

Try one of these recipes for your mood:

Relaxing massage:

- four drops of lavender, two drops of geranium, two drops of sandalwood.
- three each of rose, jasmine, geranium.
- three of chamomile, two of lavender, three of geranium.
- two of lavender, three of ylang-ylang, three of geranium.
- three of neroli, two of geranium, three of chamomile.
- four of clary sage, three of cedarwood, two of frankincense.

Stimulating, energizing massage:

- three drops of lavender, two of rosemary, one of peppermint.
- three of sandalwood, two each of cinnamon, clary sage.
- two each of lemon, rosemary, lavender.
- four of rosemary, two each of basil, clary sage.
- two each of juniper, lemon, bergamot, rosemary.
- two of basil, four of geranium, two of lavender.

Sensual massage:

- six drops of sandalwood, two of cinnamon.
- three of jasmine, three of rose, two of neroli.
- three of patchouli, five of rose.
- three each of ylang-ylang, sandalwood, rose.
- three of geranium, three of rose, two of patchouli.
- two each of ylang-ylang, clary sage, sandalwood.
- five of sandalwood, two of rose, one of neroli, two of ylang-ylang.

oil. Essential oils are highly concentrated (there are sixty thousand rose petals in one ounce of rose oil), and you only need a little for a powerful, long-lasting scent. Before using, test a drop on your skin overnight to be sure you won't have an allergic reaction. Be sure to keep the oils out of the eyes and away from children.

Essential oils enter the bloodstream through the lungs and/or the skin. Mix essential oils with carrier oils to make an aromatherapy massage oil. Add two to ten drops to a tub of warm water to perfume your bath. Fill a basin with hot water and add a few drops of oil, drape a towel over your head, and lean over the basin inhaling the fragrance. Put a drop on a handkerchief that you carry with you and inhale during the day when you need a little lift of fragrance. Dab a drop on your pillow for fragrance as you sleep. Add essential oils to lotion, cream and masks. Mix your own eau de cologne or perfume by adding essences to alcohol or sweet almond oil. Or purchase hair care products, lotions, bath oils, cosmetics and soaps that are already perfumed with essential oils.

True beauty encompasses vitality, imagination, energy and integrity.

—Jenyne M. Raines, Writer

You can scent your environment too. Mix four to six drops of essential oil with a cup of warm water in a new plant spray bottle and spritz it around the room. Light a candle and after the wax begins to melt, add a couple drops of oil to the warm wax, avoiding the wick. You can place a couple of drops on a diffuser heated by a light bulb, candle flame or electricity. In winter, add a few drops to the water in your humidifier, or place a cotton-wool ball dabbed with essential oil on a hot radiator pipe. You can place a drop of cypress, pine or cedarwood oil on a firewood log a half hour before burning. Add a drop of essential oil to potpourri and sachets.

Aromatherapy Massage •

A scented massage is a special pleasure. Rubbed into the skin, essential oils work their magic on the muscles, producing physical effects according to their specific properties. As they are inhaled, they stimulate and alter our mental, physical and emotional states and create a mood.

You can use a single essential oil, such as lavender or rose. Or you can make blends by combining compatible scents. The proper proportion of essential oil to lubricant is seven to nine drops of essence for every ounce of carrier oil. Mix the oil in small amounts to keep it fresh and potent.

Before you use a scented massage oil, check to be sure the person you're working on is not fragrance-sensitive and does not have an aversion to the scent you are using.

Never economize on luxuries.

—Angela Thirkell, Writer

Chapter 7

Bath & Spa

As recently as a century ago, a daily bath was a luxury few could afford. Now that indoor plumbing has allowed us to take basic cleanliness for granted, more people have become intrigued with the role of bathing in relaxation and health. Some are installing master baths with whirlpool bathtubs, steam cabinets and showers with pulsating spray heads. Others have discovered the pleasures of spa vacations. You don't have to spend a small fortune or take a vacation to experience the benefits of soaking and steaming. For the price of a few bath products and an hour or two of uninterrupted time, you can indulge in these bathing rituals in your own home.

Hydrotherapy has a long and varied history as a healing tradition. Soaking in hot water for relaxation has for centuries been a popular public and private ritual in Japan. Bathing with aromatic oils, salts and botanicals was thought to be a cure for whatever ailed you in ancient Egypt, Greece and Rome. Ailing and fatigued Europeans have long embarked on trips to *take the waters* at mineral hot springs in such places as Montecatini, Italy, and Baden-Baden, Germany. In Finland, the sauna is as common in the average home as the two-car garage is in the United States. Native Americans believed that mineral hot springs held spiritual power to heal illness, and they built sweat lodges for ritual purifications. They knew what they were doing: Sweating is one of the ways we eliminate toxins from the body.

There are real curative powers in fragrant hot water and steam. Baths can be both relaxing and invigorating and good for skin conditions and sore muscles. Showers dispense water massage, and the steam they create helps clear the sinuses and lungs. When you're tempted to engage in a bad habit such as overeating, nurturing yourself in the bath instead can be a luxurious way to treat your body well.

I have found the scattered parts of me and forged them all together with only two simple tools: time and hot water.

—Suzanne Chazin, Writer

Creating Your Spa • To enjoy your own home mini-spa, start by evoking a relaxing atmosphere in your bathing area with soft lighting, scented candles and soothing music. Keep your bathroom clean so it's a pleasant place to be. An inflatable bath pillow makes lounging in the bath more comfortable, and a bath tray or shower attachment is handy for storing bath supplies. Stock your bathtub or shower area with a few inexpensive accessories for cleansing and exfoliating dead skin cells: a natural sponge, sisal mitt, loofah, back scrubber and pumice stone for your feet. These promote circulation and keep your skin healthy. This might also be a good place to keep your nail brush and other nail care supplies. Stock up on some new fluffy washcloths and towels.

Don't buy just any old soap; choose cleansers that smell wonderful and keep your skin soft and smooth. If you have dry skin, you may want to try super-fatted cleansers made of olive oil, cocoa butter, vitamin E oil or aloe vera. Cleansers containing oatmeal or clay often work for oily skin. If you have sensitive skin, you may prefer soap-free liquid gels and cleansing milks.

If you have a little more to spend and want the full treatment, add a whirlpool to the tub to recreate the hydrotherapy you'd find in an expensive spa. There are also shower attachments that can give you a choice of a fine needle spray, a light mist or a pulsating massage.

Bath Basics

The best bath is warm, (85 to 95 degrees) not hot and lasts about 15 to 20 minutes. If the weather is steamy or if you want a more stimulating soak, make the water a little cooler (65 to 70 degrees). A tepid bath (75 to 85 degrees) is best before bed. After you get out of the tub, pat yourself almost dry with a towel. Seal in the moisture by smoothing a lotion or light oil over your body right away. The humectants in the lotion work by attracting moisture and holding it against your skin.

Essential Oils for the Bath

Essential oils added to your bath can relax your muscles, help you sleep, relieve pain, make you feel more alert and help clear congestion in your sinuses or chest. The chart below describes their specific properties.

Oil:	Best For:	Benefit:
Bergamot	oily skin	lifts the spirits with its spicy scent of oranges and lemons
Chamomile	dry skin, acne	reduces stress, irritability and inflammations
Eucalyptus	oily skin	relaxes the body, opens the sinuses, stimulates circulation
Geranium	oily or dry skin	uplifts, balances moods
Jasmine	dry skin	lifts depression, is calming and considered an aphrodisiac
Juniper	oily skin, acne	calms the nerves, clears respiratory and skin infections
Lavender	dry or oily skin, acne	relaxes, balances moods, is a sedative and good for skin problems
Lemon	oily skin	a tonic, invigorating with a cheerful scent
Neroli or Orange Blossom	dry skin	a sedative, lifts depression, stimulates growth of new skin cells
Rose	dry or sensitive skin	an uplifting tonic, thought to be an aphrodisiac
Rosemary	oily skin	energizes, stimulates, clears sinuses, aids mental clarity, an anti-rheumatic known to ease headaches and migraines
Ylang-Ylang	oily skin	a sedative, lifts depression, reputed to be an aphrodisiac

Bath Preparations •

You don't have to look any farther than the kitchen to find luxurious and therapeutic concoctions for your bath. Here are some simple ingredients you can use:

Salt: Salt water baths are always therapeutic. Use sea salt, and while you're in the tub, sprinkle some of it on a sponge or a cloth and scrub your skin with it to slough off dead cells and rev up your circulation. (Avoid your face and any cuts.) When you're through, rinse the salt off your body. Epsom salts are thought to speed the elimination of toxins from the body through the skin. Mineral salts, such as those from the Dead Sea, contain potassium, magnesium, calcides and other elements that are absorbed into the skin, increasing circulation and nourishing cells.

Oatmeal: For baby-soft skin, measure a cup of oatmeal into a double cheesecloth bag and whisk the bag around in the water while the water is running. Once you're in the tub, scrub your body with the bag. Your skin will feel wonderful afterward.

The **cure** for anything is salt water—**sweat, tears** or the **sea.**

—Isak Dinesen, Novelist

Milk and Olive Oil: Blend one-half cup of olive oil with one quart of whole milk or cream and add the mixture to a warm bath for a rich, relaxing soak.

Apple Cider Vinegar: A cupful of apple cider vinegar added to the bath is known to be energizing and promote muscle relaxation.

Herbs: Dried herbs can impart therapeutic benefits and often smell good too. Lavender, rosemary, thyme, mint, lemon balm, nettles and goldenrod are particularly good. Mint leaves or mint tea bags in a basin of hot water make a refreshing foot bath at the end of a long, hot day.

Brew the loose herbs—a handful per bath—as a tea, and strain the liquid into the bath. Or secure the loose ingredients in a small muslin or cheesecloth bag and let the herbs soak in a shallow amount of hot water in the tub for ten minutes, then fill the tub with warm water. You can also soak a few handfuls in a gallon of cold water for 12 hours, then heat it to a gentle boil, strain and add the liquid to the bathwater. If you have sensitive skin or are prone to allergies, test for sensitivity first on a small area of your body.

Aromatherapy Oils: To use essential oils in the bath, fill the tub with warm water and add five to ten drops of one essence or a mixture of several, dispersing the oil through the water with your hand. (If you add it earlier much of the aromatic vapor will have evaporated before you get in.) If your skin is sensitive, limit yourself to a drop or two of each essence in the bath until you see how your skin reacts.

Aromatherapy Bath Preparations: For homemade scented bath oil, mix a drop or two of essential oil with a few teaspoons of vegetable oil. Make your own scented milk bath with a tablespoon of whole milk. Create a scented bubble bath by mixing the essence with a gentle liquid soap.

Commercial Preparations: For those without the time or desire to mix their own bath potions, there are many excellent products on the market that contain herb and fruit essences, salt and oils. Bubble and foam baths are luxurious and soothing and leave skin feeling soft. Many people enjoy the sensuous feel of bath oils and bath pearls.

Other Water Treatments •

Baths aren't the only therapeutic water treatment. Showers have their uses too, especially as quick and exhilarating pick-me-ups. The rushing water and cool air stimulate the skin and create steam that clears the head and is absorbed into the skin. A nozzle with a massage setting can soothe sore or strained muscles.

A foot soak is less of a production than a full bath and can be just as energizing or relaxing. Sit on the edge of the tub and let hot water run over your feet for a minute or two. Then switch to cold water. Alternate hot and cold water for about ten minutes. Or fill up a basin with hot water and epsom salts or essential oils and soak away.

For a mini-steam treatment for your lungs and face, pour a quart and a half of boiling water into a heatproof bowl, and add three drops of an essential oil such as eucalyptus or chamomile. Then drape the towel over your head and the bowl, and inhale the steam for ten minutes.

Saunas unblock pores, remove impurities through perspiration, stimulate circulation, relieve sore muscles and make you feel more alive. Building your own home sauna is not as difficult as you might think. If you aren't interested in remodeling, you may still have access to a sauna at your gym. Alternate ten minutes in a sauna with a cool shower, then another ten minutes of sauna time, and so on. After a few rounds, you'll be rewarded with a relaxed body and mind. (If you are pregnant, have a heart condition or other relevant health problems, talk with your doctor first.) Steam rooms, often infused with the essence of eucalyptus, are also therapeutic and relaxing and will keep your lungs and sinuses clear.

Spa treatments are inexpensive therapy for body and soul. The world looks a little better and the thorniest problem more manageable after a soothing soak, tingly shower or scented steam bath.

Chapter 8

Stress & Relaxation

Sometimes big changes come all at once. You're offered a new job—a promotion! It means a big increase in pay. There's one hitch: The job is in New York, and you live in Chicago. On the one hand, you just ended a relationship, which makes it easier to go. But on the other, your dad's health is not so good, and your sister's about to have a baby. What to do? You're getting stressed out just thinking about it.

Without stress our lives would be boring—no challenges, no change, nothing to keep us interested. But many of us have more stress than is ideal. It's a constant in many of

our lives. Our society rewards high-stress lifestyles—ambition, drive, financial success and the appearance of always being busy.

It's difficult to maintain our composure when burdened by these kinds of pressures. The light of our inner beauty dims or even seems to go out completely when all of our energy is spent just trying to get through the day. We no longer project a sense of vitality to others. We have less and less to give.

We may even get sick. Medical experts estimate that 50 to 80 percent of all diseases are stress-related—headaches, ulcers, asthma, insomnia, arthritis and alcoholism are just a few. These are all symptoms of excessive strain on the mind/body system.

It's not always possible to eliminate the source of stress. When we can't remove the stress, what can we do? We can change the way we *react* to it. We can neutralize the stress by controlling our reaction to it.

One easy and effective way to deal with the onslaught of stress more effectively is to meditate. Meditation has been proven to effectively get our bodies out of this negative energy and into a state of better health and deep relaxation. It only requires a commitment of fifteen to thirty minutes each day.

Meditation is a way of slowing down enough so that we get in touch with who we are.

—Jon Kabat-Zinn, M.D., Meditation clinic director and author

Why Meditate? • Meditation has been practiced for more than two thousand years by many different religions. It is the foundation of some Eastern spiritual practices. Zen Buddhism and Indian yoga use meditation in their quest for enlightenment. Religions that do not formally advocate meditation may still evoke a meditative state in their worship. Christians practice a form of meditation when they focus their attention on a single image, such as a cross or a candle's flame. Catholic monks enter a meditative state when they repetitively chant their devotions.

But meditation offers benefits outside the spiritual realm. The act of meditating—even just thirty minutes a day—produces numerous physiological and mental changes in the human body, resulting in better health and greater peace of mind.

When you meditate, you enter a state in which you are more alert than the average person is when awake, but more profoundly relaxed than when in a deep sleep. Your breath and heart rates slow, you need less oxygen and your blood pressure goes down. You enter an *alpha* state.

Those who meditate learn to function in this relaxed physical and mental state, and often carry this over into other parts of their lives. They respond to stress better and are more alert when they need to be. Meditators have been found to be more psychologically

How Much Stress Is In Your Life?

Here are commonly recognized stressors, rated by intensity. Keep in mind that several simultaneous low-stress events can be more difficult to handle than one high-stress event. How you *react* to these stressful situations is what matters most of all.

Most Stressful

Your spouse dies

Extremely Stressful

Getting divorced
Close family member dies

Very Stressful

Getting married
Reconciling with your spouse
Getting pregnant
Having or adopting a child
Problems in your marriage
Fired from your job
Leaving the job market
Changing careers
Change in your finances
Getting ill or injured
Family member's health changes
Close friend dies

Stressful

Taking out a large loan
Defaulting on a large loan
Work responsibilities change
Trouble with your in-laws
Attaining a personal achievement
Spouse starts or stops work
Beginning or finishing school

Somewhat Stressful

Partner changes jobs
Problems with your boss
Changes at work
Taking out a small loan
Moving
Change in personal or social habits
Taking a vacation

Om

This Sanskrit word, pronounced AUM, is a mantra that has been chanted for centuries by Hindu meditators and others. It is said to be the symbolic sound of the universe, representing both the mortal and the immortal.

The lower curve of the symbol represents the dream state. The upper curve stands for the waking state. The curve extending out from the center symbolizes deep, dreamless sleep. The crescent shape at the top stands for "maya," the illusory veil of the senses. The dot represents the transcendental state. Hindus believe that when a person's spirit passes through the veil of illusion into the transcendental, she is freed from the three states.

stable and less anxious. They require less sleep and get sick less frequently. They seem to possess an internal sense of control in their lives.

Meditation serves as an antidote to "the fight-or-flight" syndrome, in which the body's systems are revved up and often get stuck on overload. It helps break the debilitating pattern of being "stressed out" that so many people experience today.

So perhaps the question becomes not "Why meditate?" but rather "What are you waiting for?"

Whenever you do something, just to do it should be your purpose.

—Shunryu Suzuki, Zen master

Meditation Basics

No matter what meditation tradition you choose, keep these things in mind:

Time and place	Meditate every day, even if you can only manage five minutes. Ideally, work up to fifteen to thirty minutes at each sitting, or more if you enjoy it. Always meditate in a relatively quiet place, with the lights low but not completely dark.
Posture	Sit on the floor or on a cushion with your back straight. Cross your legs in front of you. Another alternative is to kneel and tuck your legs under you so that your buttocks are resting on the soles of your feet. Putting a pillow under your buttocks will make this position more comfortable for extended sitting. You can also sit in a chair with your feet flat on the floor. No matter what position you choose, maintain good posture. Keep your spine comfortably straight, your chin tucked in a little and the small of your back slightly arched. Let your hands rest comfortably in your lap.
Breathing	You should always breathe through your nose rather than your mouth, especially when you meditate. Close your mouth and let your tongue rest on the roof of your mouth. Start off each meditation with a few deep breaths. Slowly fill your chest as you take in air from your abdomen. Pay attention to your breathing as you meditate. Concentrate on taking full, deep breaths.
Attitude	It's not important to do everything "right." What's important is to just do it. Accept that it is normal to have your mind wander during meditation; even the most advanced meditators experience this. You don't have to fight it. All you need to do is calmly bring your mind back each time.

Meditative Focus

• In normal life, our minds chatter constantly, even when we are not aware of it. We may be mentally focused on something we are doing, but then our minds wander: We get distracted by something else going on in the room, then we think back to an incident that happened the day before, which leads us to a thought about a future event. These "mental gymnastics" are going on inside us all the time.

Meditation teaches us to *still* our minds. It asks us to focus our attention on one thing at a time. It centers our attention within our bodies. Meditation brings us into the present moment and keeps us there.

This may involve silently repeating a mantra, focusing on our breath or concentrating our gaze on a single candle flame. Each activity brings the same result.

Meditation tames the noisy mind. Of course, rarely are we able to completely block out other thoughts—the mind is too active. Though we may not be able to stop a thought from coming into our minds, we can control whether we dwell on it or not. We have a choice. Thoughts appear, we let them go, and we resume our practice. This continued effort is what meditation is all about. And the benefits of meditation can be significant.

Benefits of Meditation

A German study showed the changes in the personalities of forty-nine people after they started practicing Transcendental Meditation.

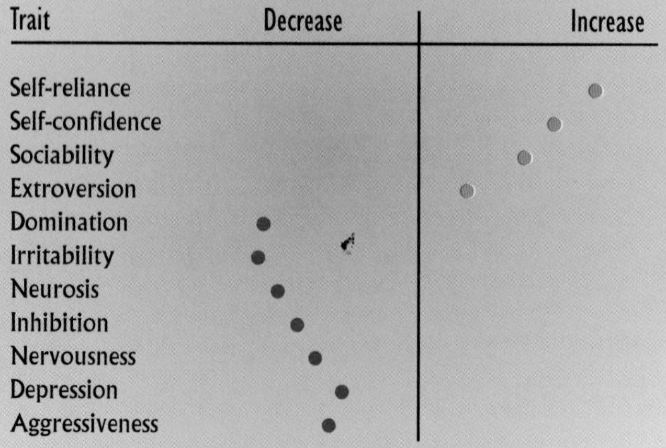

Trait	Decrease	Increase
Self-reliance		•
Self-confidence		•
Sociability		•
Extroversion		•
Domination	•	
Irritability	•	
Neurosis	•	
Inhibition	•	
Nervousness	•	
Depression	•	
Aggressiveness	•	

Three Meditations • There are many different meditation traditions, but they can be divided into three major styles: mantra, breath and object-oriented meditations.

In the mantra style of meditation, the attention is focused on a single-syllable word. Maharishi Mahesh Yogi introduced a popular version of this into the United States and called it Transcendental Meditation, or TM. A variation known as the Relaxation Response was developed by Herbert Benson of Harvard University.

Get into a comfortable sitting position, close your eyes and silently repeat a one-syllable mantra over and over, in time with your breathing. Those who attend the official TM course are given a mantra, but you can devise your own. You might try "om" or "one" or another neutral word. As with other forms of meditation, as soon as you notice thoughts, let them go and return to the mantra.

Another popular meditation practice, one that focuses on breathing, derives from Zen Buddhist practice and was introduced in the United States by D.T. Sukuzi. It is known as Zazen or sitting meditation. Zazen follows the Zen philosophy that the individual should live fully in the present moment and stay involved in everyday life rather than withdrawn. For this reason the eyes are kept open in an attentive but unfocused gaze.

Sit in a comfortable position and take a few deep breaths. Lower your eyelids but do not close them. Train your gaze downward on a fixed spot. Now follow the rhythm of your breathing, which should be as natural as possible. Keep your thoughts on your breathing. Pay attention to how it feels. Some people count their breaths as a way to concentrate their attention.

In the third type of meditation, practiced in many religions, you concentrate on an object. The type of object you choose does not matter. A lit candle is a popular choice, but it can be any object, such as a bowl, a flower or a rock. Simply gaze at the object without thinking about it in words. Keep your eyes relaxed, and take note of its characteristics. Explore the object and experience its qualities. Look at it as if you had never seen it before. When thoughts or words about the object appear in your mind, take note of them and let them go. Involve yourself in the sensation of the object, rather than thinking intellectually about it.

Good Breath • Breathing sounds like it should be the easiest thing in the world to do. But many of us do not do it correctly. When we don't breathe correctly, our brains and bodies do not get enough oxygen. Shallow breathing contributes to tense, tight muscles. Correct breathing, on the other hand, aids in relaxation.

How should you be breathing? Beneficial breathing begins with good posture. That is, your spine should be aligned so that your shoulders sit over your hips and your head follows in the same straight line, perpendicular to the floor. Your mouth should be closed. Draw in and expel breath through your nose. As you inhale, extend your diaphragm and fill the lower section of your lungs with air. Next, fill the middle section of your lungs while letting your lower ribs and chest expand slightly. Last, raise your chest a little and pull in your abdomen as you fill the upper part of your lungs. This is all done in one continuous, smooth motion. Hold the breath for a few seconds. Slowly exhale and, as

you do, pull in your abdomen slightly and lift it as you empty your lungs of air. When the breath is completed, relax your abdomen and chest.

Every now and then, or at times when you are tense, you might want to practice deep breathing. You can do it in any position. For the full effect, lay down on the floor with your knees bent, your spine straight, and your feet about eight inches apart. Put one hand on your abdomen and the other on your chest. As you inhale through your nose, let your abdomen rise completely, but only move your chest slightly. Then, open your mouth a little and gently blow out the air. Continue this routine with long, slow breaths, letting your exhalations last twice as long as your inhalations. Focus on the sound and feeling of the breathing. Do this for five to ten minutes at a time. At the end of the session, scan your body for tension. Do you feel more relaxed?

Relaxing Moment • Another way to induce calm when you're feeling tense is through progressive relaxation. In this exercise you alternately tighten and then relax individual groups of muscles. By the time you are finished, your whole body will feel much more relaxed. This is also a good exercise to practice before bed if you have trouble sleeping.

To help you get into the mood, you might want to play a tape giving directions for relaxation. Although you can buy relaxation tapes in bookstores and New Age stores, you can also make one yourself. When you create your own, you can use music you like in the background, and give the commands at a pace that is comfortable to you. If you like, use the directions below as a starting-off point for your own tape.

To begin the exercise, start by laying down on the floor in what is called the "corpse" pose in yoga: Your legs are straight and slightly apart with your toes pointing comfortably outward. Your arms are at your sides with palms up, not touching your body. Your eyes are closed. (If it is more convenient, you can do this exercise sitting down.)

Now, tense your right fist, tighter and tighter. Observe how it feels. Keep it clenched and notice the tension in your whole arm as you do. Relax it. Feel the looseness and contrast it with how it felt when it was clenched. Repeat this tightening and relaxing with the same right fist. When you are finished, do the same thing with your left fist. Progressively repeat this exercise with your wrists, then your forearms, your upper arms and your shoulders. Feel the tension and the tightness in each area and then let it go. When you relax your muscles, really let them sink into the floor.

As you tense up and relax your upper arms and shoulders, let the tension roll down your arms and out through your hands

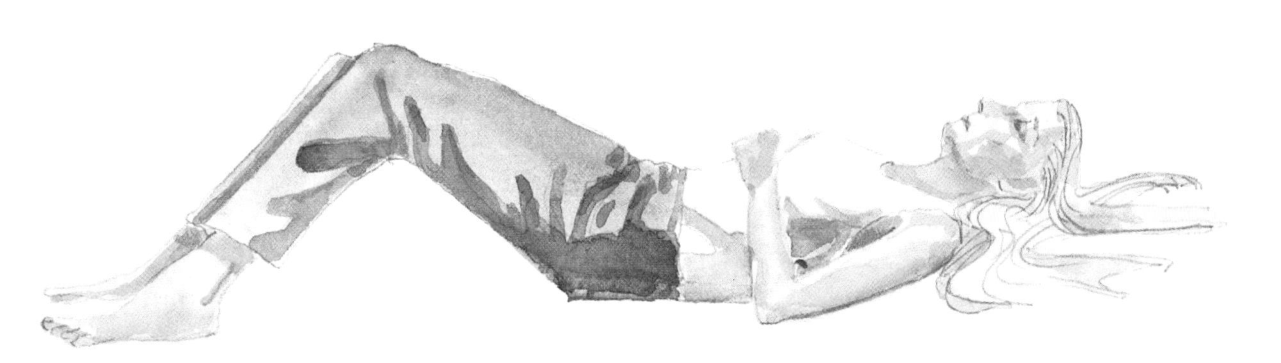

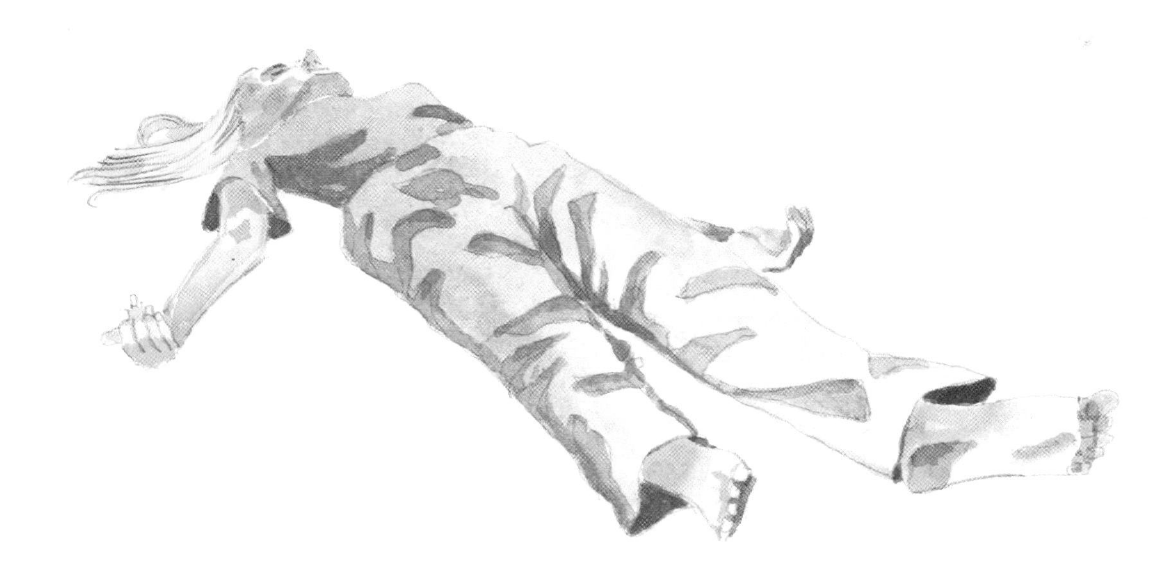

and fingertips. Your hands are relaxed, your arms are relaxed, and your shoulders are relaxed. Your whole upper body is beginning to feel more relaxed and comfortable.

Now tense up your neck muscles. This is the place where we hold the most tension. Really tighten them up. Then, relax them. Let the tension go. Let the tension roll down your neck, through your shoulders, down your arms and out your hands and fingertips. The tight muscles are giving up that tension and stress, and your entire body feels more relaxed. If you're sitting, allow your head to tip forward slightly.

Moving to the head, make a frown with your forehead. Tighten up those muscles as much as you can. Now relax and smooth them out. Allow your forehead and facial muscles to relax. Just let those muscles go. Close your eyes tightly and squint. Focus on the tension, then let it go. Relax your eyes. Let them remain closed. Now clench your jaw, really tighten it up. Relax your jaw. Your lips will be slightly parted. Tighten your lips into an "O." Now relax them. As you do, notice that your scalp, forehead, eyes, jaw and mouth are relaxed. Your whole body is relaxed.

Alternately tighten and relax every part of your torso now. Shrug your shoulders, then relax them. Tighten your chest and notice how that feels. Hold your breath in, then exhale. Tighten your abdomen, your stomach and your inner organs. Then let them go. Tense up your pelvic area and buttocks, hold it for several seconds, then relax. Take a few deep breaths. Then move down the legs, alternately tightening and relaxing: your thighs, your knees, your calves, your ankles, your feet, your toes.

Feel the relaxation now in your whole body. The body feels heavy. All tension flows out of you. Every part of you is now relaxed.

All things share the same breath.

—Chief Stealth, Duwamish Tribe

Wake-Up Call

In Hindu mythology, Indians worshipped the sun god as a symbol of health and immortality. They honored the god by practicing the sun salutation every day at sunrise. As they performed each of the twelve positions they chanted a different mantra or name for one of the god's special qualities.

The sun salutation is still a yoga staple. It's a wonderful way to get a complete, whole-body stretch first thing in the morning. Do it in one continuous, flowing motion, building up to twelve rounds.

1. Stand straight with your feet together and your palms in a prayer position in front of your chest. Exhale.

2. Inhale as you raise your arms up and stretch backward from the waist. Tighten buttocks as you lean back. Push the hips out and keep your legs straight and your neck relaxed.

3. Exhale and press your palms down on the ground, fingertips in line with your toes. Bend your knees if necessary.

4. Inhale as you bend your knees and slide the right (or alternately, the left) leg back, resting the knee on the floor. Arch your back and look up, lifting your chin.

5. Retain your breath, and bring the other leg back. Support your weight on your hands and toes. Keep your head and body in a straight incline and look at the floor between your hands.

6. Exhale as you lower first your knees, then your chest and finally your forehead to the floor. Keep your buttocks up and your toes curled under.

12. Exhale as you gently return to the original standing position and bring your arms to your sides.

11. Inhale as you stretch your arms forward, up and back over your head. Stretch back slowly from the waist, pushing hips out and keeping legs straight.

10. Exhale as you bring the other leg forward, raise yourself up and bend down from the waist. Keep your palms down and your fingertips in line with your toes.

9. Inhale as you step forward and place the left (or right) foot between your hands. Rest your hands on the floor and look up, lifting your chin.

8. Exhale as you curl your toes under, raise your hips and pivot into an inverted "V." Push your head and heels down if you can and keep your shoulders back.

7. Inhale as you lower your hips, point your toes and extend back, raising your forehead, nose, chin, chest and ribs. Keep your legs together and shoulders down.

Chapter 9

Healing Touch

As infants, many of us are lavished with generous amounts of affection. We are held, nuzzled, kissed, stroked, rocked and caressed. But as we get older, the touch decreases to less frequent hugs and hand holding. By adolescence, when our sexuality emerges, touch tapers off even further. As adults, we get most of our physical affection from our sexual partner, with our children, pets and a friend's occasional hug filling in the gaps. Some people go without regular touch at all.

But we never lose our need for physical contact. Touch makes us feel loved, secure, happy and healthy. Without touch, infants die. Doctors at the turn of the century,

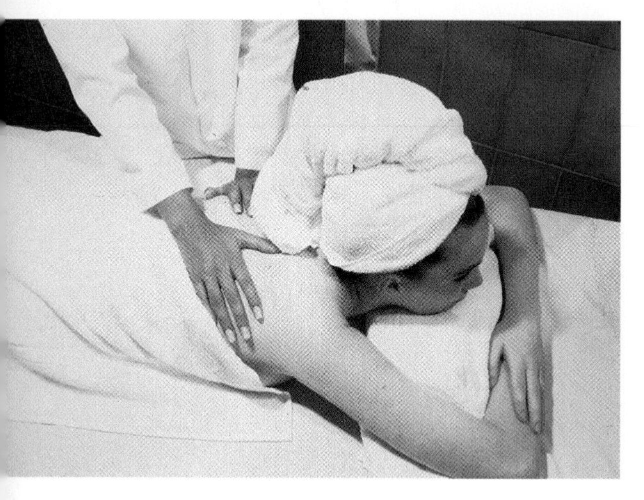

investigating the high mortality rate in orphanages, found that infants suffering from no other malady would die if they were deprived of physical contact. It has been proven that children grow up healthier and better adjusted when they have a steady diet of physical touch. As adults, touch contributes to our sense of well-being and gives us pleasure and joy. When it's lacking in our lives, we may unknowingly try to satisfy or anesthetize our need for it through overeating, drinking, drugs or promiscuity. It's much better just to go to the source of our desire and get our daily quota of life-sustaining touch.

Maybe you are one of the lucky ones whose life is rich with physical contact. If not, try slowly increasing the level of affection you express to your friends and family. Start small, with a playful pat on the arm, a comforting hand on the shoulder or a quick affectionate hug. You may feel awkward at first. But after a while, touching those you care about in a gentle, affectionate way will seem as natural to you as eating and breathing.

Healthful Massage • Whether getting a simple rubdown or a full shiatsu treatment, the benefits we receive from touch are multiplied when we are the recipients of a massage. A good massage leaves us feeling both more relaxed and more alert. It soothes sore muscles and relaxes an anxious mind. It cleanses the body of toxins, stimulates circulation and relieves stress. It aids the body's ability to heal itself.

Massage speeds up the movement of oxygen-rich blood from the heart to the

Massage has been slow to catch on in this country because people cannot believe that something which feels so good can be good for them.

—Bruria Ginton, Writer

extremities and back again. After five minutes of massage, the oxygen content of all rubbed tissue has increased 10 to 15 percent. Massage also encourages the drainage of lymph from the muscles. Lymph filters bacteria, toxins and other wastes through nodes in the neck, armpits, groin and knees, and circulates with the compression of muscles and our breath. Massage aids the process.

Massage makes sore muscles feel better. Muscles tighten when we are worried or tense and stay contracted. Lactic acid builds up in these tightened muscles, making the area stiff, sore and painful when we are touched. Because massage relaxes the muscles, these wastes are released much more quickly.

Massage also makes pain much easier to bear. Have you ever found yourself unconsciously rubbing a shin when you've knocked it against something? There's a reason for it. When we rub the skin we stimulate touch receptors which send impulses to the brain that close the pain gateways. In effect, rubbing an area that hurts stops the pain message from getting through.

A massage to the face, scalp and neck can often cure a headache and relieve tension. Massages to the hands, arms and shoulders feel particularly good to those who work on computers or do other work with their hands. A foot massage, using reflexology or just basic massage strokes, feels great at the end of a long day.

While it's true that massage appears to have incredible healing powers, it may not be for everyone. Who should avoid massage? Anyone with an illness, high fever, inflammation, skin rash, swelling, bruises, sprains, broken bones, burns or varicose veins. Also seek medical guidance if there is heart disease, circulatory problems, pregnancy, diabetes, acute back pain, cancer, epilepsy, HIV, AIDS or undiagnosed illness or disease.

Power of Touch

When we touch others, even in the most unobtrusive way, we make them feel better about us. Waitresses participating in a study in Oxford, Mississippi, were told to lightly touch some diners on the hand or shoulder. Customers who were touched consistently gave the waitresses higher tips. In a Boston experiment, a woman repeatedly left money at a phone booth, then returned when someone picked it up. Ninety-six percent of those that she touched in a subliminal way when she asked about the money returned it to her. Just 63 percent of those she did not touch returned it.

A Long History • Americans have been slow in accepting massage as a legitimate therapeutic treatment, but it has been an integral part of medical practices in Asia, the Middle East and Europe for centuries. Massage is thought to be the oldest form of medicine known to humanity.

Massage is mentioned in *The Yellow Emperor's Classic of Internal Medicine,* published in 2598 B.C. in China. In the eleventh century B.C., the Arab philosopher-physician Avicenna wrote that massage could "disperse the effect matters found in the muscles and not expelled by exercise." In fact, the word *massage* originated with the Arabic word *massa,* meaning *to touch.* In India, Sanskrit texts carved into the temples show reliefs of Buddha receiving massage treatments.

In the East, massage known as acupressure originated in China. In this system, vital life energy circulating through the body along meridians or pathways is manipulated using the same principles that form the basis of acupuncture. The Chinese introduced acupressure to the Japanese 1,000 years ago. The Japanese called it *shiatsu,* which means *finger pressure.* Shiatsu massage was introduced into the United States in 1953.

Massage also has played an important role in Western medicine. Greek and Roman physicians recommended it as part of a health care regimen that included exercise and mineral baths. Homer's *Odyssey* mentions it as a therapy for exhausted heroes. Hippocrates, the Greek physician considered to be the father of Western physical medicine, insisted that it be made a part of physician training. "The physician must be experienced in many things, but most assuredly in rubbing," he said. Roman gladiators used massage as preparation for wrestling with lions. Julius Caesar used massage to control his epilepsy.

In the Middle Ages, massage largely fell from favor in Europe because of repressive attitudes toward the body. The Swedish fencing master and gymnastics instructor Per Henrick Ling is responsible for the revival of interest in massage in the nineteenth century. After traveling through Asia, Ling devised a system of massage therapy based on what he had seen in Asia and his own knowledge of physiology and holistic health. His program became known as the Swedish style of massage.

While Europeans embrace Swedish massage wholeheartedly, even covering it in their national health insurance programs, Americans did not really catch onto it until recently. In the last thirty years, massage therapy has finally been accepted as a credible profession in the United States, with the number of schools and practitioners increasing annually.

Popular Techniques • Swedish Massage is the most common type of massage practiced in the United States today. This is a system of using long strokes, kneading and friction on the superficial muscles—always directed toward the heart—combined with movements of the joints. Used on the whole body, it promotes relaxation, improves circulation, increases range of motion and relieves muscle tension.

Another popular form of massage, the Japanese Shiatsu, is a variation of acupressure that originated in China. It is sometimes described as acupuncture without needles. This Japanese acupressure technique uses the fingers (*shi*) to apply pressure (*atsu*) on special points along twelve meridians, or pathways, along which circulates vital life energy (*chi* or *ki*). Blocked energy along these meridians can cause physical illness. Shiatsu is said to release the clogs, rebalance the energy flow and restore health.

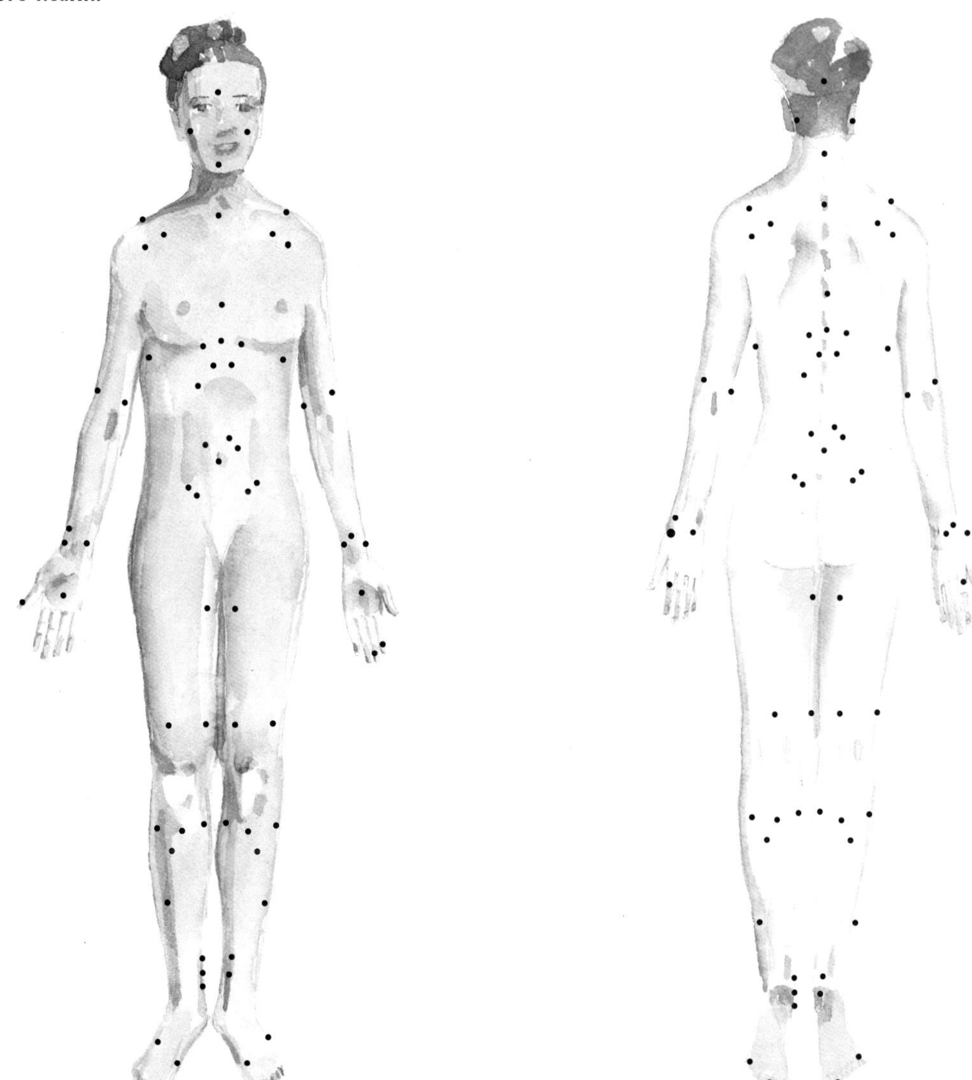

In Reflexology, principles of acupressure and shiatsu are applied to the hands and feet, where pressure points on the surface are thought to correspond or *reflex* to other areas of the body. Energy travels from these points to the corresponding organ through meridians, which begin in the feet. Stimulating these points is said to promote better circulation to the corresponding area, drain wastes, aid in the organ's functioning, as well as drain tension from the body and break up waste deposits in the feet.

The Deep Tissue Massage method releases chronic patterns of tension through slow strokes and deep finger pressure on tight areas, either following or going across the grain of muscles, tendons and fascia. This restores muscle suppleness and length. It may be used on a specific area or for a full body massage.

Sports Therapy may incorporate any of the massage styles, but focuses on deep, gentle pressure to muscles used in a particular sport or activity. Stroking goes in the direction of the heart. This therapy is designed to benefit muscles by warming and softening tissue, realigning muscle fibers, helping to heal scar tissue and flushing toxins from specific muscles.

The more high technology around us, the more the need for human touch.
—John Naisbitt, Futurist and writer

Trigger Point Therapy was developed by Janet Travell, M.D., specifically for dealing with pain. Concentrated finger pressure is applied to trigger points or irritated areas in muscles to break the cycle of spasm and pain. Trigger points are small, very sensitive areas in the muscle fibers that develop under extreme physical stress, commonly in the lower back, neck and shoulders. When these key points in the muscles are manipulated, muscles relax automatically.

Hydrotherapy uses water for therapeutic benefit with hot packs, ice applications, saunas, steam baths, hot showers and whirlpools. Cold water is used for injury and hot water for muscle relaxation. Water has a soothing effect and can act as a light massage in whirlpools.

Rolfing/Structural Integration was developed in the U.S. in the late 1930s by Ida Rolf, Ph.D. This is a form of deep, often painful, muscular manipulation and massage designed to realign the body to its proper structural posture and relieve physical and emotional tension. It is based on the idea that repressed traumatic experiences from the past cause unconscious muscle tension that moves the body out of its natural alignment and vitality into a state of overall inflexibility and gravitational imbalance. Besides limiting movement, the muscle tension causes restriction of circulation and inefficient organ function.

Giving a Massage

You might hire someone to give you a massage, but you can also get one from a friend or partner, or give one to someone else or to yourself.

A soothing, safe ambiance sets the stage for a pleasurable massage experience, whether indoors or outside. Take the phone off the hook, dim the lights or light candles and make sure the room temperature is agreeably warm. If giving a massage outdoors, find a private, comfortable area. Set up the massage area with sheets, blankets, towels, pillows and cushions. Stock the compact disc or tape player with relaxing, lightly rhythmic, instrumental music (piano, harp, flute) or nature sounds.

The person getting the massage should lie on a firm, padded surface, either a thigh-high table (a massage table or makeshift substitute) or the floor. Put a long piece of egg crate foam underneath them for padding. It's best not to give a massage on a bed, which is too soft, unless you are giving your partner a gentle, stroking massage before sleep.

The best lubricant is light, cold-pressed vegetable oil, with a capsule of vitamin E or teaspoon of wheat germ oil added to preserve the lubricant and prevent oxidation. Popular choices are safflower, grape seed, soy and sunflower oils. Others are peach kernel, jojoba, avocado or sweet almond, which are rich in vitamins A and E. Other alternatives include sesame, which is light and nutty in scent, and coconut, with its

Time Out

Concerned about stress among their employees, a growing number of companies are providing on-site massage or "mini-massages." Workers remain fully clothed and receive fifteen minutes or so of acupressure-type massage on shoulders, neck, arms and back while sitting on a stool or a specially designed chair. Apple Computer, Merrill Lynch and the Dallas Herald Tribune are among those who have offered it.

reminder of the beach. Some people favor a massage cream. Avoid mineral or baby oils and regular hand lotion.

Store the oil in a bottle with a flip top and pouring nozzle so it doesn't spill when you need a few drops for the massage. Another option is to pour some oil into a small bowl to dip into during the massage.

Before beginning the massage, take a bath, do some deep breathing or meditate for a few minutes to get yourself into a relaxed mental state. Put on loose, comfortable clothing. Cover the person getting a massage with a sheet or towel for comfort and warmth. Expose each area of the body only as you are ready to work on it.

Before you begin, warm up your hands by running them under hot water and rubbing them together vigorously for a minute or two. Get into a comfortable position that doesn't strain your back. Pour a few teaspoons of oil into your palm and let it warm up (or keep the oil container in a bowl of hot water). Then spread it slowly over the body area by stroking it on until you have enough for your hands to glide smoothly.

Work rhythmically and intuitively, starting with long, complete movements. Match strokes gently to your breathing. Face in the direction you're stroking for ease of movement. Pay attention to how your partner's muscles feel. If they are tight and knotted in one place, such as the shoulders, give that area extra attention. Vary your touch by changing the speed of the strokes or the pressure of your hands. Ask for feedback as you go along, and make sure your partner tells you if something is painful. Use repetition to relax muscles rather than pressing harder than is comfortable for you or your partner. Keep constant contact, smoothing your hand down the body as you go from neck to feet or gently keeping your hand resting in one spot as you shift positions. Experiment with different kinds of massages. You can start with a relaxing massage to the back and shoulders.

Hands are messengers of **emotion.**

—Diane Ackerman, Author

Benefits of Massage

Massage lays claim to some pretty impressive benefits. Here are some you might expect when you get a massage.

Physical

- Deep relaxation and stress reduction
- Relief of muscle tension, spasm and stiffness
- Greater joint flexibility and range of motion
- Deeper and easier breathing
- Better circulation of blood and lymph fluids
- Reduced blood pressure
- Relief of tension-related headaches or eyestrain
- Healthier, better nourished skin
- Improved posture
- Faster healing time from pulled muscles and ligaments
- Strengthened immune system and disease prevention

Mental

- Relaxed state of alertness
- Reduced mental stress, a calmer mind
- Greater ability to monitor stress signals and respond

Emotional

- Satisfaction of the need for caring and nurturing touch
- Feeling of well-being
- Greater ease of emotional expression
- Enhanced self-image
- Reduced levels of anxiety
- Sense of being unified and in harmony

Different Strokes

The following are the basic strokes used in massage. Each of them can be varied in any number of ways and applied with light, medium or heavy pressure for different effects.

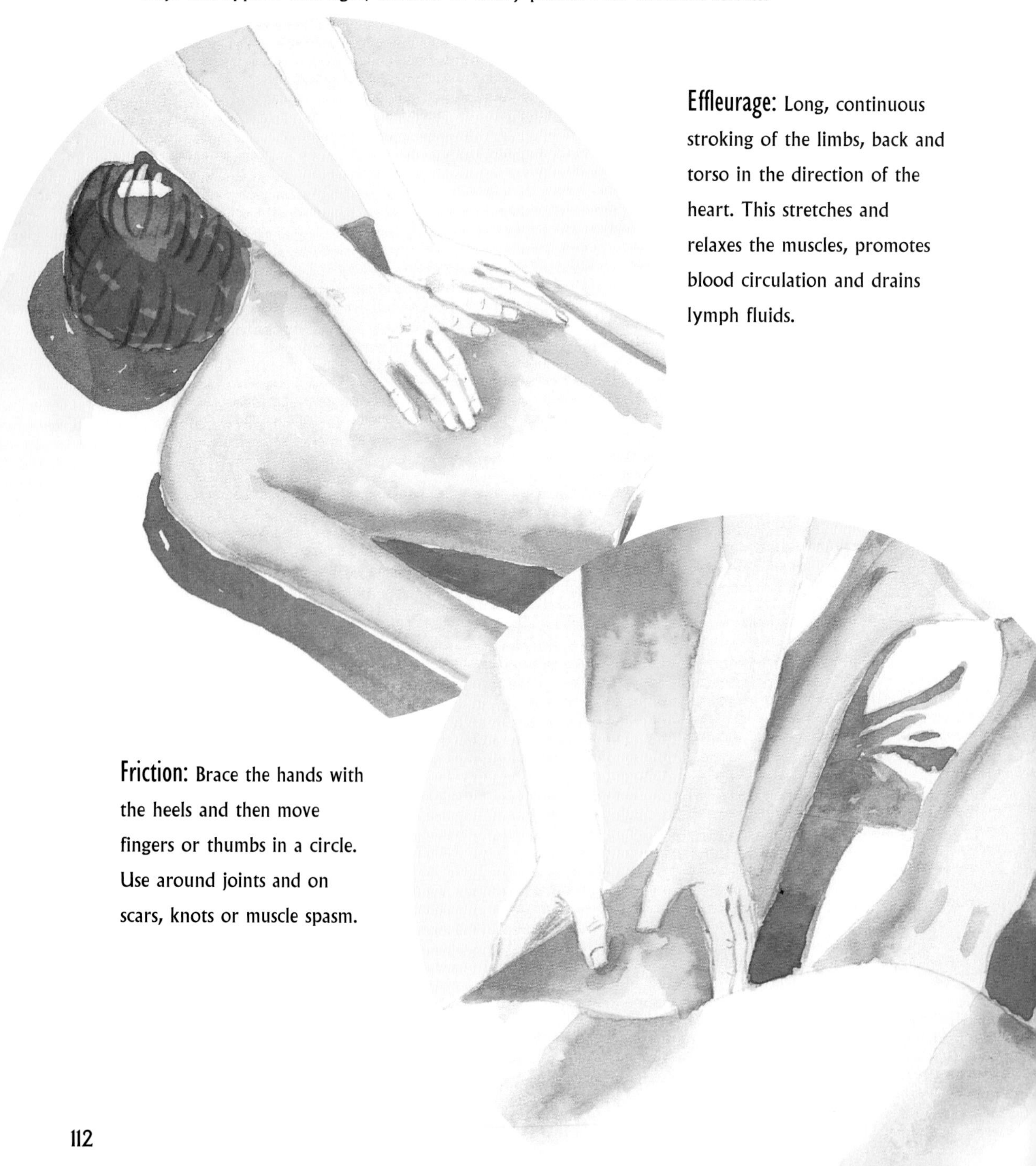

Effleurage: Long, continuous stroking of the limbs, back and torso in the direction of the heart. This stretches and relaxes the muscles, promotes blood circulation and drains lymph fluids.

Friction: Brace the hands with the heels and then move fingers or thumbs in a circle. Use around joints and on scars, knots or muscle spasm.

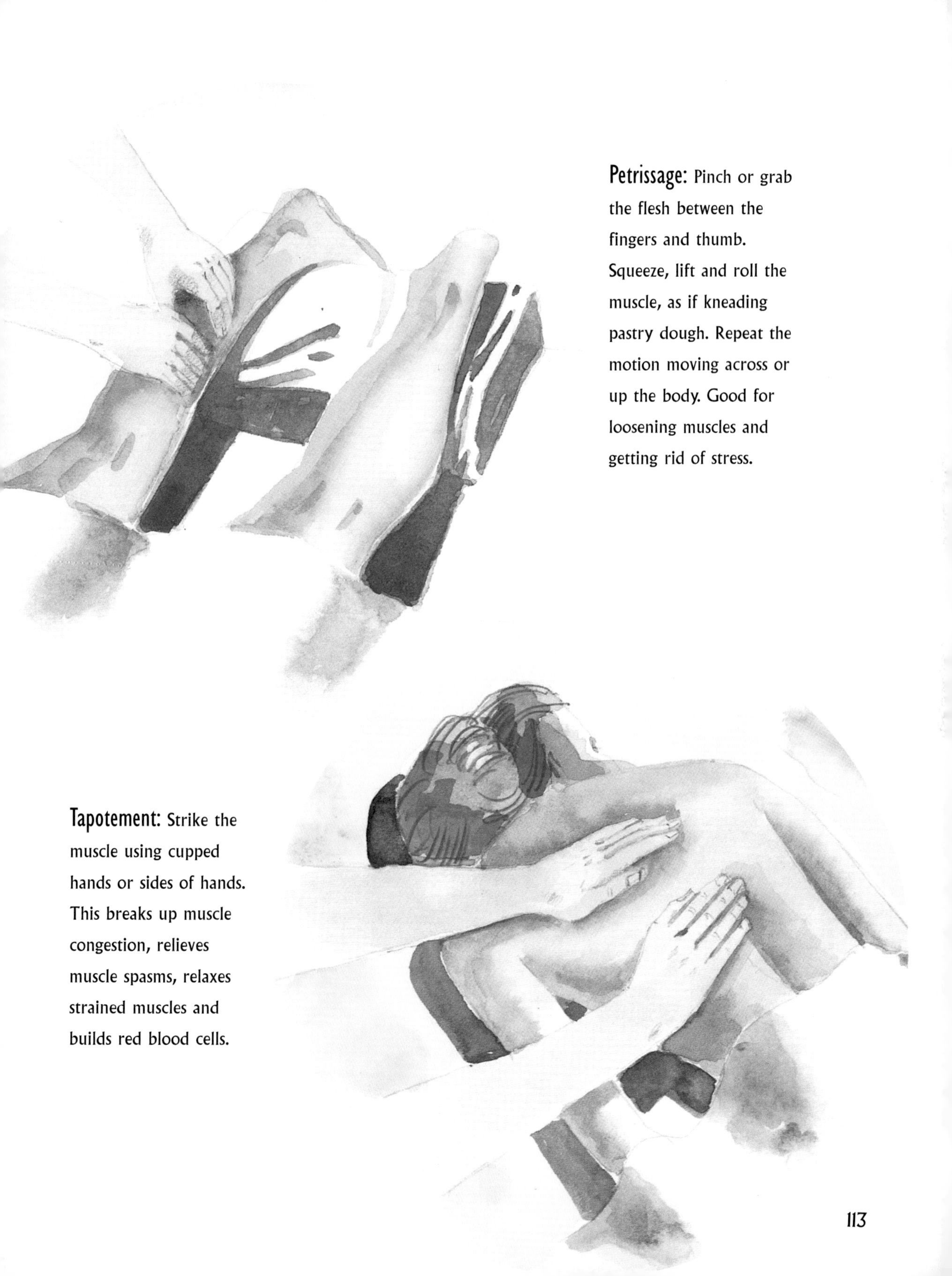

Petrissage: Pinch or grab the flesh between the fingers and thumb. Squeeze, lift and roll the muscle, as if kneading pastry dough. Repeat the motion moving across or up the body. Good for loosening muscles and getting rid of stress.

Tapotement: Strike the muscle using cupped hands or sides of hands. This breaks up muscle congestion, relieves muscle spasms, relaxes strained muscles and builds red blood cells.

Different Strokes (continued)

Pressing: Apply a gentle but firm downward pressure on the tissue with the thumbs, fingertips, heel of your hand or entire palm. This loosens tight areas.

Circling: Keep palms flat and fingers together. Make small firm circling movements with your hands moving up or across the body. Hands moving in unison can go in opposite directions or move together.

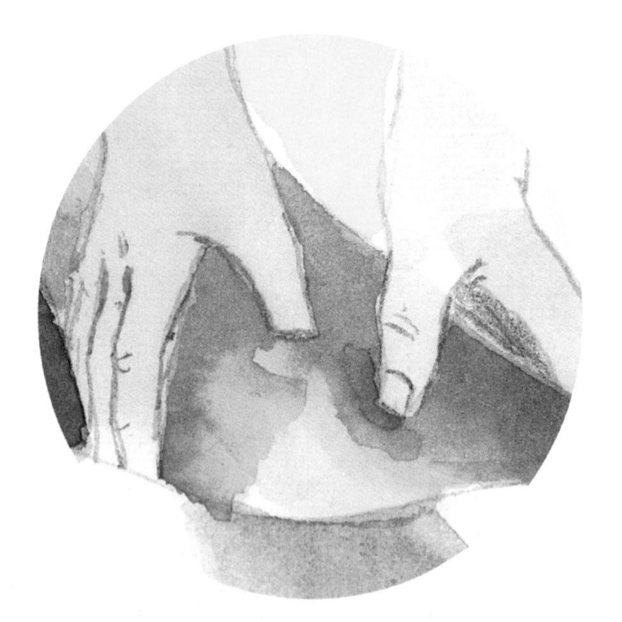

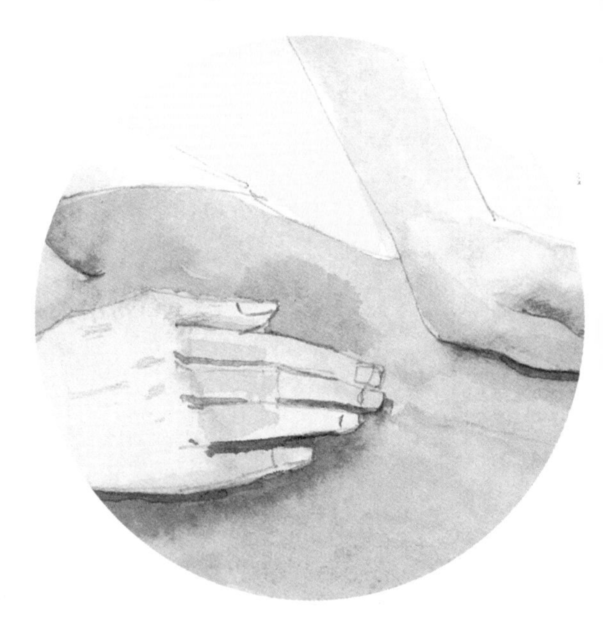

Wringing: Position hands with fingertips away from the direction you are working. Pull one hand toward you and follow it with the other. Repeat with a fluid motion. Use along the sides of the torso, limbs or other areas with loose flesh. Stimulates nerve reaction and blood flow.

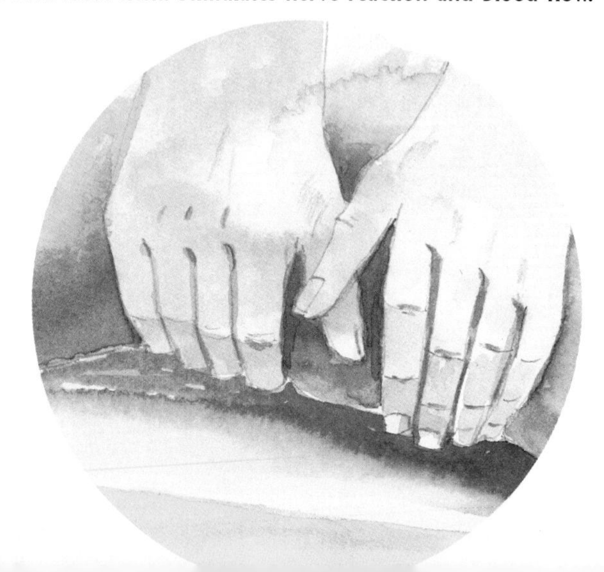

Finding a Professional Even though you have acquired the soothing techniques to give a relaxing massage, someone might not always be there to reciprocate. Today, you no longer need to go to questionable massage parlors or hippie retreats to get a massage. Chances are there may be a talented massage therapist practicing right in your neighborhood or near your workplace.

Start by asking people you know if they've used anyone they like. You can also check the telephone directory's business pages; look for those that advertise therapeutic massage. Other places to find bodyworkers include:

- chiropractic, medical and physical therapy offices
- health clubs and fitness centers
- massage schools
- spas, salons and resorts
- massage association referrals
- local health publications
- bulletin boards of health food and New Age stores
- on-site at trade shows, sporting events, in supermarkets and offices.

Selecting a massage therapist is partially a matter of looking at qualifications. Find out if they have been certified by a nationally accredited massage school. Are they licensed? (Nineteen states offer licensing, which requires at least 500 hours of training.) What techniques do they use? What do they charge? (Average prices range from $40 to $60 an hour; $50 to $100 if they come to you.)

Try out a few until you find someone you like. Massage is more than technique—it's an intuitive ability to heal and connect. As Shane Watson, owner of Southern California's Bodywork Emporium says, "It's all in the gift of touch."

Massage Tools

Whether you're giving yourself a massage or practicing on someone else, massage tools can come in handy. They can help you reach difficult spots and save the strength in your thumbs and fingers. Joan Johnson, author of *The Healing Art of Sports Massage,* recommends the Thera Cane, a fiberglass bar with wooden knobs for massaging the back, neck, shoulders,

arms and legs; the Knobble, a rounded wooden device for applying deep pressure to trigger points; the Thumbsaver, a small wooden ball with a projecting rubber knob for direct pressure-point massage; and the Foot Massage, a wooden dowel with raised, hard plastic bumps, designed by a reflexologist. Most cost between $5 and $30 and are sold in bodywork shops or through advertisements in massage and health magazines found in health food or New Age stores.

Back Massage

1. Place your hands at the base of the back on either side of the spine, with your fingers pointing toward the head. (Never apply pressure to the spine itself.) Slide your hands up the back until you reach the neck. Then slide the hands firmly across the shoulder and glide them down the outside of the back. As you reach the lower back, pull them together and repeat the motion several times.

2. Move your hands to the sides of the body. Starting from the hips on one side of the body, begin to knead the muscles, pulling away from the bone. Work up the sides of the torso and across the tops of the arms and shoulders. Change to thumbs and fingers when you reach smaller areas, but do not pinch. Move to the other side and repeat.

3. From the base of the spine, make small circular movements into the muscles on either side of the spine with your thumbs until you reach the neck. Apply the same motion to the muscles around the shoulder blades.

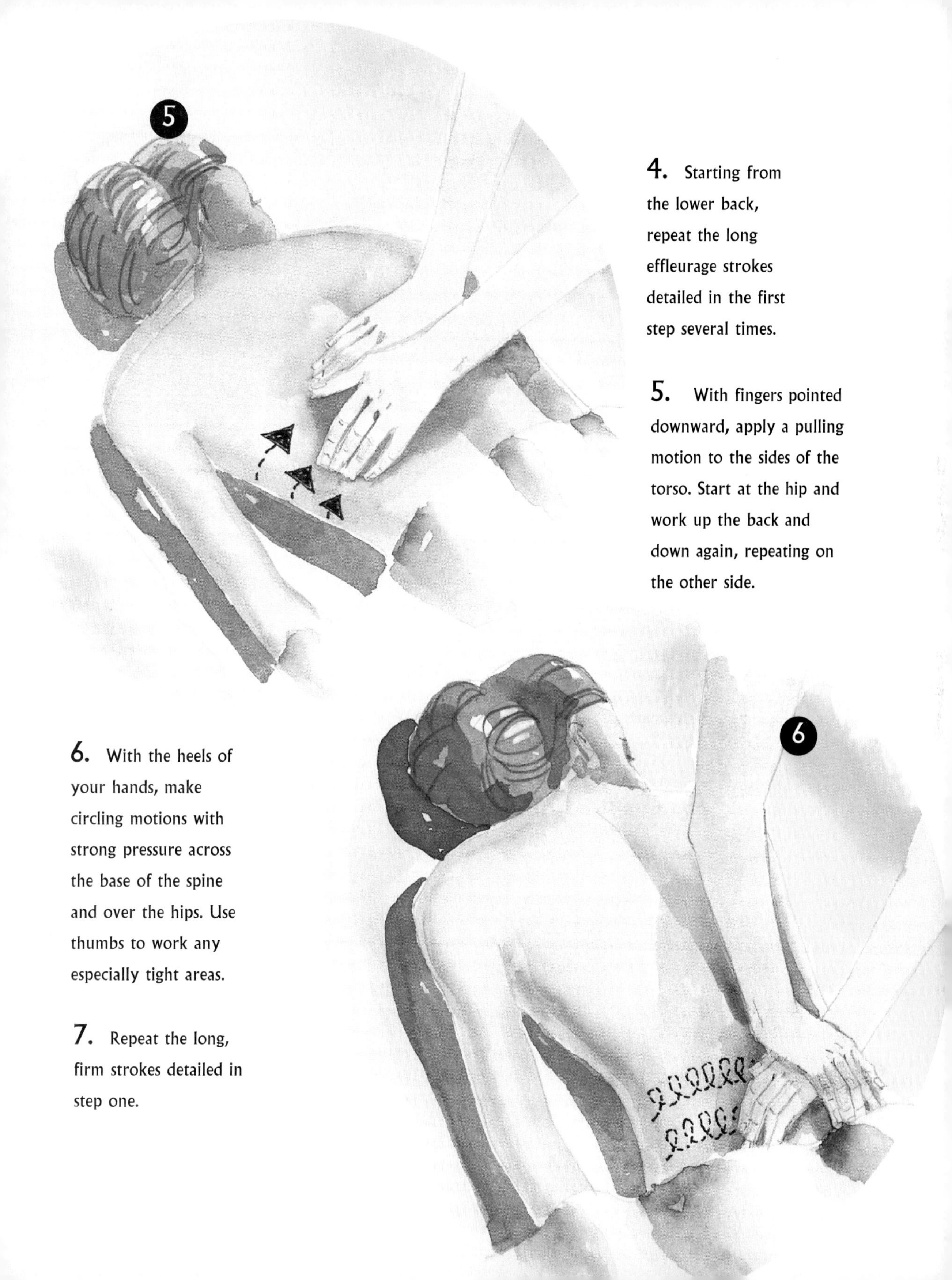

4. Starting from the lower back, repeat the long effleurage strokes detailed in the first step several times.

5. With fingers pointed downward, apply a pulling motion to the sides of the torso. Start at the hip and work up the back and down again, repeating on the other side.

6. With the heels of your hands, make circling motions with strong pressure across the base of the spine and over the hips. Use thumbs to work any especially tight areas.

7. Repeat the long, firm strokes detailed in step one.

8. Gently knead the shoulders.

9. Shape your hand as if it were a claw and place it on the shoulder blade. Rotate the skin over the shoulder blade several times to the right and left, repeating on both sides.

10. Place your hands side by side, horizontally, in the middle of the back. Simultaneously slide one hand to the left shoulder and the other to the right hip, stretching the back. Repeat the motion, with your hands going to the right shoulder and left hip.

I don't fear anything I don't understand. When I start to think about it, I order a massage, and it goes away.

—Hedy Lamarr, Actor

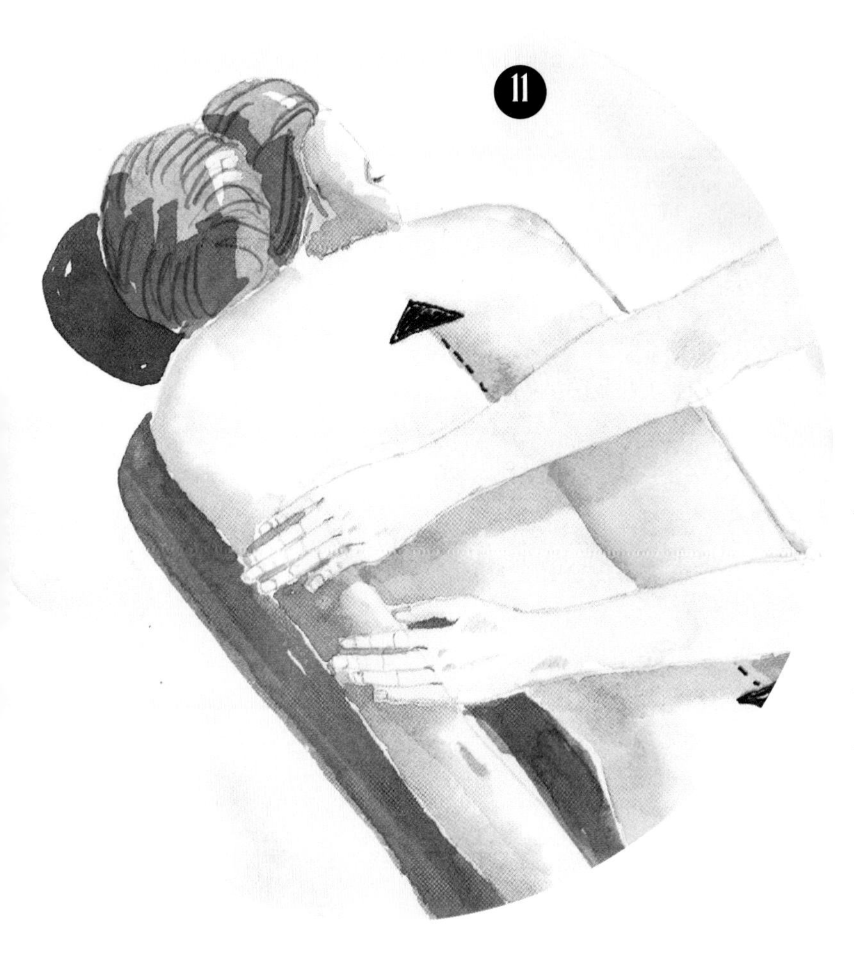

11. Place both arms horizontally across the back in the center, and slowly but firmly slide them apart. Move one to the shoulders and the other to the tops of the buttocks, to stretch the back.

Chapter 10

Skin & Makeup

Beautiful skin is a prized quality, and understandably so. When we meet others face to face, it is among the first things people notice as we make eye contact and shake hands or embrace. Skin is the contact point where our inner and outer worlds meet.

Skin has amazing properties. It protects our bodies from infection by secreting antiseptic substances that fight off invading microorganisms. It prevents moisture loss and regulates temperature. Our skin protects our tissues and organs from abrasion and other injuries. It shields the body from dangerous ultraviolet rays in sunlight. It also is a highly

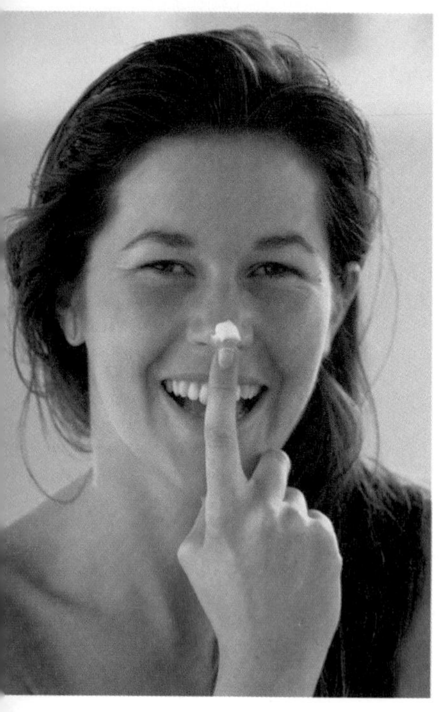

sensitive organ that responds to outside stimuli, including touch, pressure, pain and pleasure.

Our skin is a permeable covering that is influenced by both our inner health and the exterior conditions to which it is exposed. For beautiful and healthy skin, start with the basics of sleep, nutrition, exercise and relaxation. Why are these important? During sleep our skin repairs itself. Nutrition provides proteins, fats, vitamins and minerals for its regrowth. Drinking plenty of pure water is essential, as it is the source of our skin's moisture. Exercise encourages the elimination of toxins through sweat and stimulates blood circulation that nourishes the skin. Relaxation helps keep our emotions on an even keel, preventing skin disturbances and reducing the tense muscles and frown lines that no amount of makeup can hide.

Then comes topical care. Each day our skin comes into contact with ultraviolet radiation, dirt, smoke and pollution. These mingle with the oils, perspiration, salts and toxins that our skin exudes, as well as the dead skin cells that are continually being shed. Proper cleansing, exfoliation, toning, moisturizing and sun protection are the final ingredients of a healthy, vibrant complexion.

Skin Basics •

Skin care products should be strong enough to clean and help the skin retain moisture, but gentle enough to protect the acid mantle, which is composed of oil (sebum) and sweat (urea). This natural acid pH balance is what guards the skin against acne infections and irritations.

Trial and error is often necessary to find the products that work best for your skin. Cost doesn't necessarily make a difference in quality: Inexpensive creams and cleansers often have the same ingredients and work as well as pricier potions. Look for a product that gives you a good result and feels and smells good to you. Using skin care products from which you derive sensual enjoyment is another way you can nurture yourself every day.

Cleansers and Toners •

A skin cleanser should be used at night to remove dirt, toxins and makeup from the day. Gentle water-soluble cleansers that do not dry out the skin or leave it feeling greasy are usually better than soap. Apply gently with your fingers, a sponge or a washcloth, and rinse your face thoroughly with warm or tepid water.

Taking joy in life is a woman's best cosmetic. —Rosalind Russell, Actor

Toning with a gentle astringent after you cleanse will help refresh the skin and eliminate oiliness and cleanser residue.

AHAs and Exfoliators • Alpha-hydroxy acids (glycolic or lactic acid) are natural ingredients extracted from sugarcane, fruits and sour milk. These skin exfoliants work by dissolving the *glue* between dead skin cells, allowing the old skin to peel off, unclogging pores and revealing the smooth skin below.

AHA products are helpful for those with dry skin, because they peel off the excess dry, flaky skin that typically builds up. They are also a boon for those with oily skin, because they remove the dead skin cells that block pores and trap oil inside, causing blackheads and blemishes. Both skin types improve with increased exfoliation.

The bottom line? AHAs can improve the look and feel of your skin, reduce fine lines and help moisturizers absorb more effectively. AHAs are found today in moisturizers, masks and other skin care products.

Masks and scrubs (both AHA and non-AHA) may also act as exfoliants, which can be used once a week or more depending on your skin. Always apply gently in a circular motion and rinse off completely with warm water.

Moisturizers and Antioxidants • Lotions, oils and creams attract and hold moisture in the skin, preventing the premature effects of aging. They form a barrier that protects the skin from the elements, environmental pollution and the drying effects of central heating and air conditioning.

Your need for moisturizer varies with your age, your skin type, the season and the time of day. Always choose one that does not irritate your skin or clog pores. Lighter lotions are generally better for the face, for they allow the skin to breathe.

Melanoma Alert

Melanoma is the fastest-growing type of cancer, affecting about 32,000 Americans in 1993. The skin cancer is triggered by ultraviolet radiation exposure from the sun and is signaled by the growth or appearance of an irregular mole. If caught early, melanoma is completely curable with the mole's removal. However, the cancer can spread if it is not caught early.

Early detection is everything. Those with blonde or red hair should be especially vigilant. Examine your body once a month for moles that have changes in size, thickness or color. Other

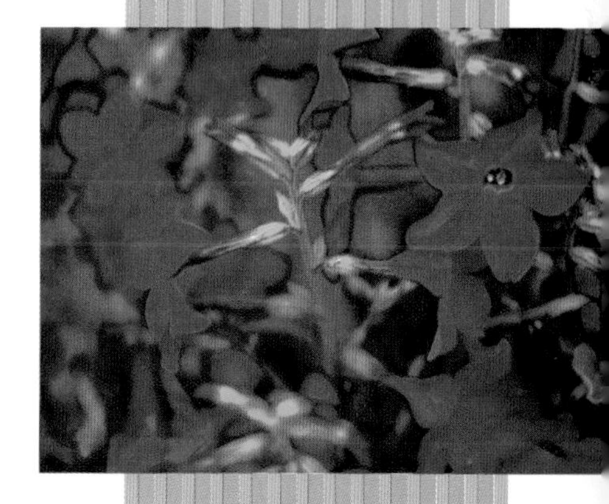

characteristics to watch for are asymmetry, ragged edges, bleeding, itching or pain. If you have a mole that looks suspicious, have it examined by a dermatologist immediately.

Beauty Roots

Since at least as far back as the Egyptians in 1400 B.C., generations of women (and often men) have used makeup and lotions to enhance the skin's beauty. They lined their eyes with kohl pencil, applied ground minerals such as lapis lazuli on eyelids, and rubbed roots on their cheeks to stain them.

Earlier generations also battled blemishes, wrinkles and the drying effects of sun and wind. The list of things they used—honey, oils, fats, milk, fruits, vegetables, vinegar and grains—is not very different from those we incorporate into our beauty products today. The second-century Roman doctor Galen devised a cold cream of oils, wax and scented water—essentially the same formula we use today.

Apply moisturizer in the morning, after cleansing and before putting on makeup. You can use a moisturizer with an SPF (sun protection formula) 15 sunscreen or apply sunscreen separately. At night, you may like to use a moisturizer that contains alpha-hydroxy acids. If you have oily skin, you may want to moisturize only around the eyes or not at all.

Moisturizers now contain many nutrients and additives to prevent premature aging of the skin. Among these are antioxidants, including vitamins A, B, C and E. Antioxidants *eat up* free radicals, unstable oxygen molecules from UV rays and pollution that turn iron to rust, make apples brown and cause skin to age. Antioxidants halt free-radical damage and are thought to be instrumental in protecting the skin.

Sun Protection •

After good health care and a nonirritating cleansing routine, protection from the sun is the most important ingredient for beautiful skin. Premature wrinkles are caused by sun exposure. Rather than waiting until skin damage has been done, then turning to plastic surgery and skin peels to fix it, start with prevention. That means using SPF 15 sunscreen with UVA and UVB protection daily. Make it a part of your morning routine.

If you can normally stay in the sun for 20 to 40 minutes before you begin to burn, an SPF of 15 will allow you to stay there 15 times longer before you burn—five to ten hours. The type of day and time of year, as well as the altitude and your age, can make a difference in a sunscreen's effectiveness. Don't forget to apply it to your lips, ears, hands, neck, hairline and the tops of your feet. Be sure to reapply lotion when swimming or exercising.

Other sun-protection tips: Stay out of the sun between 10 a.m. and 3 p.m., especially during the summer months. Make it a habit to wear hats in the summer, and other coverings if you have fair hair and skin. Avoid tanning salons. Be sure to cover your lips, ears, back of the neck, hairline and tops of the feet. Wrinkles are caused by sun exposure, genetics and illness.

If you do accidentally burn, cool compresses soaked in equal parts milk and water will soothe the skin. Aspirin or ibuprofen can help ease the pain. Apply fresh aloe vera gel to stimulate the healing process.

Recipe for Success •

Each skin type responds better to some commercial skin care products and natural ingredients than others. Oily skin needs lighter moisturizers and ingredients that remove excess oil. Dry skin needs richer moisturizers and ingredients that add oil. When you're looking for products for your skin type or making your own homemade masks, cleansers or toners, choose ingredients recommended for your skin type.

Normal skin has fine pores and soft skin that doesn't feel excessively oily or prone to pimples. Natural products for this skin type include sweet almond oil, apricot oil, yogurt, buttermilk, sour cream, papaya, lemon juice, oatmeal, eggs and cucumber. Chamomile, comfrey, elderflower, fennel and rose are all-round good skin tonics.

Oily skin is shiny and coarse with large pores that may be prone to blackheads and acne. Any products you use should remove oil without irritating or overstimulating the oil glands. Natural products that can benefit your skin type are brewer's yeast, almonds, honey, oatmeal, citrus juices, egg white with mineral water, witch hazel and herbs such as calendula, yarrow, horsetail, sage, elderflower and nettles.

Lemon juice and egg white applied to blemishes can help control blackheads and tone skin. Diluted apple cider vinegar can help restore the skin's acid balance.

Dry skin is delicate, thin and prone to fine lines and flakiness. It requires gentle care, mild cleansing and light oils or lotions for moisturizing. Use natural ingredients such as yogurt, brewer's yeast, egg yolk, honey, almond oil, wheat germ oil, olive oil, avocado, coconut oil, oatmeal, rose water, chamomile and comfrey.

Combination skin has some oily areas (usually around the nose, mouth and chin) and other areas that are dry or normal (the cheeks and around the eyes). Use ingredients that are specific to the needs of each area.

Sensitive skin is dry, fine and prone to rash, broken capillaries and allergies. This skin type requires especially gentle care. Honey, yogurt, fine oatmeal and cucumber may be best. Chamomile, coltsfoot, rose, fennel, comfrey, elderflower, marshmallow root and borage can be soothing.

Cycle of Life

Birth to 20

Description: Skin is pristine at birth. Tanning and burning in the early years can add up to trouble later in life. In adolescence, oil production increases and blemishes may flare up.

Recommendations: Always protect skin from the sun with an SPF 15 sunscreen to avoid tanning. Establish a gentle, regular cleansing routine, healthy eating and sleeping habits and get plenty of exercise in the teen years. See a dermatologist if acne becomes a problem.

The 20s

Description: Skin eruptions have often settled down, and skin may be at its prime—soft, supple and wrinkle-free.

Recommendations: Continue to wear sunscreen and stay away from tanning. A cleansing and moisturizing routine is important, especially if you are wearing makeup. Use an exfoliator, such as an alpha-hydroxy acid product or gentle scrub, if your skin responds well. Establish healthy sleep, exercise and eating habits, which pay off later on.

The 30s

Description: Wrinkles and age spots begin to appear, and tiny lines start to develop around the eyes. Hormones from pregnancy and oral contraceptives may cause some skin discoloration. Skin starts to look less radiant.

Recommendations: Regular use of moisturizer, especially for those with dry skin, becomes important now. Continue to guard against sun exposure with a sunscreen; protect your neck and hands as well as your face. AHA products can help keep skin looking vibrant and smooth. Maintain a regular exercise program, and make getting enough sleep a priority.

Though good looks may rally one's attention,

The 60s

Description: Wrinkles and sagging due to age, rather than sun damage, start to show up now. Your face, neck and hands are in better shape if you have practiced a lifetime of good health habits and protected your skin from the sun.

Recommendations: Continue to cleanse, moisturize and wear sunscreen. A positive attitude, enthusiasm for living and concern for others will help you stay youthful looking.

The 50s

Description: Wrinkles and sagging increase, while cell renewal decreases dramatically. Skin becomes thinner and retains less water.

Recommendations: Continue moisturizing face, neck and hands religiously, switching to cream cleansers and heavier moisturizers if needed. Keep up regular exercise and other good health habits.

The 40s

Description: Collagen and elastin decrease and the skin becomes dryer. Lines and wrinkles become more prominent. Blood circulation slows, leaving skin and lips with less of a blush.

Recommendations: Moisturizer is especially important now. AHA products and other exfoliators help increase skin-cell turnover. A change in makeup application may be appropriate. Stay physically active, but always wear sunscreen when outdoors and remember to drink lots of water.

a lasting sense of a person's beauty reveals itself in stages.

—Diane Ackerman, Author

Easy Makeup

Putting on makeup doesn't have to be a time-consuming project. Consider these simple steps.

1. Check your eyebrow area for stray hairs. To shape the brow, line up a pencil from the bottom of the nostril to the inside of the eye. This is the point where the brows should begin. Line up the pencil with the nostril and outside of the eye for the outer brow point. Avoid overplucking.

2. Cover up dark shadows under the eyes or blemishes with a thin layer of concealer in a shade slightly lighter than your face tone.

3. Use a cosmetic sponge to lightly spread and blend a layer of foundation or lightweight tint over your face. Dilute the foundation with water if desired.

4. Close your eyes and dust a fine layer of powder over your face with a makeup brush to set the makeup and eliminate shine.

5. Groom and fill in eyebrows with a powder and a brow brush or a brow pencil. Use light, feathery strokes.

6. Apply a light, neutral-toned eye shadow over the eye area from the lashes to the brow. Add darker shadows to the lid, crease or corners of the eye to highlight and recess areas.

7. Line your eyes with a dark powder shadow and eye liner brush or liner pencil. Start on the outer corner of the lower lid and work in to the middle to a point that is most attractive for your eyes.

8. Apply a mascara that doesn't smear, clump or flake.

9. Apply blush, following the hollow or *apple* of your cheekbones and blending in circular movements to avoid a harsh stripe.

10. Outline lips with liner or pencil and fill in with lipstick.

Nail Care

Details make a difference in your appearance, as they do with everything else in life. Keeping your nails groomed is an important finishing touch in your beauty routine. Give them regular attention—weekly cleaning, trimming and filing. If you wear polish, be sure to keep it fresh, removing it before it starts to peel.

Fingernails

1. Trim nails with a nail clipper.
2. File nails into desired shape—squared off, oval or combination—with an emery board, going in one direction only.
3. Soak nails for a few minutes in lukewarm water with a little liquid soap.
4. While they are soaking, clean nails with a nail brush.
5. Remove from water and dry hands lightly.
6. Apply a rich lotion or almond oil to cuticles.
7. Push back cuticles with an orangewood stick.
8. Massage hands with a rich hand lotion.
9. Buff tops of nails to give them a shine.
10. Apply polish if desired.

Toenails

1. Cut toenails straight across with a nail clipper.
2. File edges smooth with an emery board.
3. Soak feet for a few minutes in a basin of warm water and a little liquid soap or Epsom salts.
4. While feet are soaking, clean nails with a nail brush.
5. Use a pumice stone or buffer to remove dead skin from bottoms and sides of feet.
6. Remove feet from water and dry thoroughly.
7. Massage almond oil or lotion into cuticles.
8. Push back cuticles with an orangewood stick.
9. Massage oil or lotion into feet.
10. Buff nails, being careful not to irritate the skin.
11. Apply polish if desired.

Brushing Up

Toss out the foam applicators and tiny blusher brushes that come with your makeup. Your best makeup investment is a supply of professional-quality application brushes. With their rounded, soft edges, they make blending easier and help you create a more natural look. You can find them at cosmetic counters and cosmetic supply stores. The basic brushes are:

eye-liner brush	to trace a line of color around the eye
eye-shadow brush	to apply and blend colors above the eye
eyebrow brush	to color and groom the brow
blusher brush	to dust color on the cheeks
lip brush	to fill in lipstick color and line lips
powder brush	to set makeup with a fine layer of powder

Fresh Face

Keep track of your makeup purchases and replace a product when it is too old. To prevent infections, mascara should be discarded after a few months, liquid foundation after two years and powdered eye shadow after four years. Buy makeup in small quantities, and store it in a cool, dark place.

Finishing Touch • Makeup can highlight our best features, but it can't make up for poor health habits or a grim disposition. If you're feeling tense, anxious or stressed-out, start your makeup routine with a minute of deep breathing, stretches and head rolls. Allow the muscles in your face, neck and shoulders to relax.

The time you spend putting on makeup in the morning can be a quiet time you use to prepare yourself for the day. You literally get ready to *face* the world. Organize yourself so you have a few minutes to devote to yourself and your appearance before you leave the house.

Makeup should enhance your natural beauty. Not everyone wants or needs to wear it, but it does give a finished look to a woman's face. It can smooth out uneven skin tone, add dimension and play up your best features. Apply makeup with a light touch, for you want people to notice you, not your eye shadow. "Approach makeup the way you do food," says makeup artist Shu Uemura. "Always stop when you're 80 percent full."

Every now and then set aside an hour to sit in front of the mirror and try out a new look. A professional makeover can also be helpful in learning how to use makeup to your best advantage. Pay attention not only to what products and colors the stylist chooses, but how they are applied. As you get older and move into different stages of your life, your makeup needs to change too. Every face benefits from different techniques, colors and products.

Remember that what is true about skin care products is true about makeup as well: The quality of the product does not necessarily increase with the price. There are excellent products in all price ranges. Experiment and find out what works best for you.

Nature gives you the face you have at twenty;

it is up to you to merit the face you have at fifty.

—Coco Chanel, Fashion designer

Chapter 11

Our standards of hair care have improved tremendously over the centuries. It used to be thought that washing hair was unhealthy. In the Middle Ages, French court women covered their heads with enormous hairpieces and only washed their hair once or twice a year. It wasn't until the eighteenth century that regular hair washing came back into favor.

Today we consider cleanliness one of the most important attributes of beautiful hair. We admire hair that is shiny, vibrant and natural looking, for this reflects a state of health and well-being.

Many of us are not happy with the hair we were given. Those with curly hair often wish it were straight, and those who have straight hair wish it had more curl. If we have fine hair, we want it to be more substantial, and if we have thick hair we wish it were less so. The color never seems to be what we want. So we alter our hair in whatever way we can—curling it, straightening it, coloring it and adding body.

All textures, types and colors of hair can be equally stunning with the proper care. The most important step in hair care is regular and gentle cleansing and conditioning. This is especially true when we subject hair to blow-dryers, heat curlers and chemical processes. To sacrifice the intrinsic quality of our hair to achieve a color or style would be to miss the point of hair care completely, which is to protect and highlight our natural gifts.

Hair Composition •

Hair is primarily made of protein, along with a small amount of amino acids, minerals and trace elements. It consists of three layers: the cuticle on the outside, then the cortex and the medulla inside. The cuticle is made of transparent, overlapping scales that protect the inside layers and give hair its sheen. The cortex and medulla are rows of cells growing side by side that give hair its flexibility, strength, width and color.

Most hair care products work on the cuticle—coating it with oil or stripping oil off, smoothing it down so that it reflects light or roughing it up so that the edges lift and separate, grabbing other strands and giving hair a fuller appearance. When the cuticle is intact, the hair has luster and shine. When it is damaged, hair becomes dry and brittle.

There are 100,000 to 150,000 hairs on the average head, about 1,000 in every square inch. Each hair develops in a follicle, a cavity in the skin in which the root is housed. Capillaries and nerves feed the growing hair, which is made of cells that rapidly reproduce. As these cells reach the surface, they die and harden into a strand of hair. The hair is pushed out from the surface of the skin as its cells multiply.

This growth phase lasts between two and six years, during which time a hair grows about a half-inch per month, or six inches a year. Then hair cells stop reproducing, and the root is released from the follicle and slowly moves up to the surface of the skin. Soon a new hair begins to grow and pushes the old hair out. We lose about fifty to one hundred hairs each day. Much more than that, and it might mean a problem with the root due to rapid weight loss, stress, poor health or damage caused by a hair treatment. If no hair is lost, it may be that follicles are clogged by excess oil and dead skin, and the hair needs more frequent washing.

Proper Care •

Hair can be washed every day or once a week, depending on the individual scalp and hair. Normal hair can be washed daily or whenever needed. If hair is oily, every other day might be fine. Be careful not to overwash, which stimulates the oil glands further. Dry hair might be washed and conditioned once or twice a week, with special attention paid to the scalp.

Before washing, brush dry hair to loosen dirt and gently comb out tangles. Wet the hair with warm water and pour a small amount of shampoo in the palm. Rub it into the hair at the hairline in front and continue to the ends, working across the temple and crown. Using the fingertips, make small circles, working up a lather. Add a little water if necessary. Gently massage the scalp to stimulate blood circulation to the follicles and remove dead skin cells. Then smooth your hands through the hair to remove the excess suds. Rinse shampoo from hair with warm to tepid water until the water runs clean, from three to five minutes. Repeat if hair is especially dirty, or if you use a lot of hair spray or styling gel.

If you use a conditioner, pour a small amount into the palm and rub it into the ends of the hair first, working up. If the scalp tends to be oily, avoid the roots. Comb the conditioner through your hair with your fingers. Let it sit on the hair for three to five minutes before rinsing with warm and then cool water.

After washing and conditioning, blot excess water from hair with a thick towel, taking care not to rub it too vigorously.

Damage Control

The secret to healthy, undamaged hair is to treat it as gently as possible. Brush or comb hair as infrequently as possible, and use a soft brush. Start at the top and work down, being most gentle with the ends. Avoid brushing wet hair, and never wring or twist hair dry with your hands. Instead, squeeze it dry gently using a towel or your hands. When blowing hair dry, avoid the direct application of heat. Keep the nozzle three to six inches away.

Hair is more prone to damage when it is wet. Comb hair with a wide-toothed comb or fingers to remove tangles. Apply styling mousse or gel to hair. Dry hair naturally when possible, or blow-dry at a low to medium temperature. When blow-drying, part your hair into sections. Starting at the bottom, lift hair with a brush, comb or fingertips and direct the dryer toward the roots. Work your way up to the crown, shaping hair into the style you prefer. Let each section cool before releasing hair from brush so that it holds its shape. If you like, finish with a spritz of hair spray.

Remember to wash your combs and brushes regularly so you don't reapply oil and dirt to your hair when styling. Apply a small amount of shampoo to each and soak in warm water. Comb loose hair from the brush and rinse thoroughly.

Cleansers and Conditioners •

Shampoos are designed for different hair types and have specific ingredients added to treat specific problems. Some shampoos add extra body to fine hair, strength to chemically damaged hair and oils to dry hair. It pays to choose a shampoo designed with your hair type and condition in mind.

Dry hair, for example, can benefit from a shampoo with emollients and conditioners. For oily hair, use products without conditioning agents. For fine hair, be careful not to overcondition—it will weigh hair down. Coarse hair can take a lot of conditioner.

The first two ingredients in any shampoo are typically water and a detergent, needed to remove excess oil and dirt from hair. It is the finishing ingredients that vary and give each shampoo its particular quality. A shampoo may contain oils that reflect light and give hair shine, humectants that attract moisture to the hair, herbal and plant extracts for fragrance and conditioning, or chemicals that restore hair's acid balance. Products for chemically processed, color-treated and dry hair contain emollients, proteins, amino acids and oils that bind to the shaft. Those that add body, volume or thickness contain amino acids, panthenol and glycerin, as well as styling agents. Shampoos that reduce

If only I'd known that one day my differentness would be an asset, my early life would have been much easier.
—Bette Midler, Actor and singer

frizzies bind the cuticle down with silicone oil, guar or cellulose.

When choosing a shampoo, keep in mind the needs of your scalp as well as your hair. You might have a dry, flaky scalp with normal hair or an oily scalp and fine hair. Choose a shampoo for your scalp that will not be a problem for your hair. If your hair needs a conditioner, but your scalp does not, avoid conditioning the roots.

Conditioners contain humectants, which attract and hold moisture into the hair so it remains soft. Finishing agents leave a film on the hair that makes it feel soft and look shiny. Emulsions coat the hair shaft and increase body. Conditioners may also contain sunscreen, color enhancers and protein.

Detanglers lubricate individual hair strands so there's less friction between them, while defrizzers block the hair's ability to absorb extra moisture.

Styling products apply a sticky layer on the cuticle that adheres to other hairs, helping hold the hair in place. Of these, mousses are lightweight foams that add lift and body, while gels offer a firmer hold and a slick look. Sculpting and styling sprays set hair in place.

Style Considerations • Your choice of hairstyle gives people you meet quite a bit of information about you. Does your current

Styling Tools

- Wide-toothed comb for detangling and styling
- Rat-tail comb for styling
- Assortment of brushes, such as a round styling brush and a curved vented brush
- Long metal hair clips to hold waves in place
- Bobby pins or small metal hair clips for pin curls
- Blow-dryer with diffuser and directional attachments
- Electric curlers, regular rollers
- Curling iron or two for different sizes of curls
- Hand mirror to look at the back of the head
- Hairpins and hair sticks for upswept hairdos such as chignons
- Elastic bands, headbands, ribbons, barrettes and combs

hair style accurately reflect who you are? Does it flatter the shape of your face and work well with your hair's unique qualities? These are the sorts of questions to consider when choosing your next hairstyle.

Hair Quality and Texture: Is your hair straight, wavy or curly, fine or coarse, thin or thick in quantity? Your best results will come from working with, rather than against, your hair's natural qualities. Straight and fine hair is ideally suited to a blunt cut, for example, while thick and curly hair looks good in layers.

Body and Head Size: Hair should be proportional to the size and height of your body. A general rule of thumb is that the taller you are, the longer the hair you can comfortably wear. Those who are 5'4 and under look best with short or medium-length styles. Women with smaller faces do better with cropped hair with bangs or a fringe that frames the face, especially when they have fine features and a nicely shaped head.

Head and Body Shape: Is your body angular or curvaceous? Is your face shape angular or round? Your most flattering hair style will complement the shape of your face and body. A blunt cut picks up the angular lines in a person's face and figure, as does hair pulled straight back, worn with straight bangs,

> It is possible that blondes also prefer gentlemen.
>
> —Mamie Van Doren, Actor

Face and Hair

One of the main considerations when choosing a hair style should be the shape of your face. Each facial type is most flattered by certain styles and lengths of hair.

Facial Shape:	Description:	Best Styles:
Oval	Balanced proportions and softly rounded outline.	The most versatile type. Can wear a softly curved or more angular hair style.
Round	Curved and almost as wide as long.	Emphasize curves with a soft hair style. Add height or fullness on top and minimize the sides by brushing hair forward or using fringe to frame the face. An off-center part is flattering.
Oblong	Long and narrow.	Emphasize the soft lines, but play down the length of the face with bangs, no extra height and a chin-length cut. Layered cuts are uplifting, compared to long, straight hair which makes the face appear longer. Add fullness to the sides of the hair and try an off-center part.
Rectangular	Long and angular.	Emphasize angles of the face with a geometric cut or asymmetric style. Use bangs and no fullness or height on top. Part hair off-center.
Square	Wide with strong jaw and cheekbones.	Emphasize the angles with a geometric cut and asymmetric styles. Add height and use off-center bangs. Minimize the sides.
Diamond	Wide or high cheekbones with a narrow forehead and chin.	Emphasize the cheekbones with angular hair styles. Add width across the forehead with fullness or bangs.
Pear	Narrow, long forehead with wide jaw.	Emphasize soft curves. Add fullness across forehead with soft curls to balance narrow forehead and onto cheeks to soften and diminish cheek width. Layer through the crown to lend fullness to the top.
Heart	Wide curving forehead and temple with a narrow chin.	Emphasize the curves and add fullness and feathering at chin line to widen a narrow chin. Use an off-center part to soften the forehead.

or cut into an angular silhouette. Those with curved facial and body lines can wear hair wavy, curled or cut with a rounded silhouette.

Lifestyle and Personality: Are you active and sporty? If so, you may need a casual, easy-care cut. Do you spend your free time entertaining in style and thus need a look that's more sophisticated? Does your profession require a conservative look or a looser, more casual style? What haircut will flatter the style of clothes you usually wear? Does your personality lend itself to a dramatic style or something softer? Is your age a factor in the length of hair you should wear? In general (and there are exceptions to this rule), long hair looks better on younger women, especially when it is worn down.

Maintenance: Are you handy with a curling iron and hot rollers or are you all thumbs? Do you have little time to devote to hair styling and drying or can you take whatever time it requires to get it right?

A Cut Above •

There's no substitute for a great haircut. It makes styling easier. Well-cut hair falls correctly and looks good whether you spend five or fifty minutes styling it.

The way to get a great haircut is to find a talented haircutter. In looking for a talented stylist, keep your eyes open for people who have the same type of hair as you and a haircut you admire. Ask who their stylist is. Most people will be flattered and happy to share the information. Or if you're interested in a particular salon but aren't familiar with its stylists, get a manicure there first and observe how each haircutter works.

Stay away from a stylist who gives you the latest look without regard to how it looks on you. You should trust a hairstylist to give you flattering cuts appropriate to your facial shape and lifestyle. Make sure the person cutting your hair listens to you.

It can be a challenge to communicate what you are looking for. Start by showing up for the appointment in the types of clothes you usually wear, either at work or play. If you need a particular type of cut for work, wear work attire to the appointment so the stylist can get a picture of the image you want to convey. Come to your appointment early and flip through photo books in the waiting area for pictures of the cut you want. Or bring magazine photos you have clipped or a picture of your hair when it was cut in the style you want now.

Be prepared to discuss the work that has been done on your hair previously—the date of your last color treatment and permanent, for example. If you are pregnant or nursing, tell the stylist; you should avoid chemical work at this time.

Color Basics •

People have been coloring their hair for thousands of years with wine, roots, flowers and ash. The first chemical dye was patented in Paris in 1883 and was based on a technique used for dying textiles. In 1907, L'Oreal sold the first hair colorants to salons in France. Today half of all women over 25 color their hair.

When might you consider coloring your hair? If you want to highlight or enrich your natural color, hide the gray or change your look completely. There are several methods of coloring, ranging from rinses that give a very temporary film of color to permanent methods that change color completely.

Temporary rinses are just that—temporary. They wash out in one to six shampoos, which makes them ideal for trying out a new shade before making a permanent change. They cannot lighten your natural color, but will subtly brighten or highlight your own color, neutralize the yellow in white and gray hair, or reduce ash or red tones.

Semi-permanent colors can enrich your natural color but not lighten it. They wash out after about a dozen shampoos as they only coat the outside of the hair. Use them to intensify your color, darken it by a shade or hide a small amount of gray. They can also be good for testing a new color or highlight.

Demi-permanent or intermediate colors deposit dye in the hair shaft and last as long as permanent colors, but do not produce as great a change. They can be used to match your natural hair color and give it more depth or cover up to half of the gray. They last four to six weeks before hair grows out.

Permanent color removes color from the cortex, swells the hair shaft allowing dyes to enter and then deposits a new shade. You can lighten or darken your color by about two shades or levels with permanent color. You can also add intensity or shine to your existing color and cover gray. Even "permanent" hair color fades over time and must be retouched every four to six weeks, depending on the hair color and how fast your hair grows.

Herbal rinses impart color as well. Chamomile is often used for blonde highlights, as are marigold leaves, lemon juice, orris root and elderflowers. For brown highlights, clove and coffee can be effective. Henna adds red or orange tones, while blue malva neutralizes the brassiness of gray.

The color, intensity and tone you choose are very important. Keep in mind when you are choosing a color that it must work with your skin and eyes. If you make a dramatic change in your hair color, be prepared to follow through with some changes in your wardrobe and makeup. Do a test on a small strand or section of hair before coloring the whole head.

In determining your best colors, work from your natural color. Consider its intensity—light, medium or dark. Unless you're going for an unnatural look, your new hair color should be only a shade or two away from your original color. Determine if your natural hair is *warm* or *cool.* Warm shades fall into the *autumn* and *spring* color categories and have highlights of red, copper, auburn or gold. Cool colors are *winters* and *summers* and have ash, muted or bluish tones in their hair. It's important that you stay within your tonal family.

Hair appears to have been designed to protect our heads from the elements and prevent heat loss. We also use it to attract sexual partners and signify our place in the world. But hair serves a purely decorative purpose too. Hair is a canvas upon which we can express our individuality, using color, curl, ornaments and creative styling.

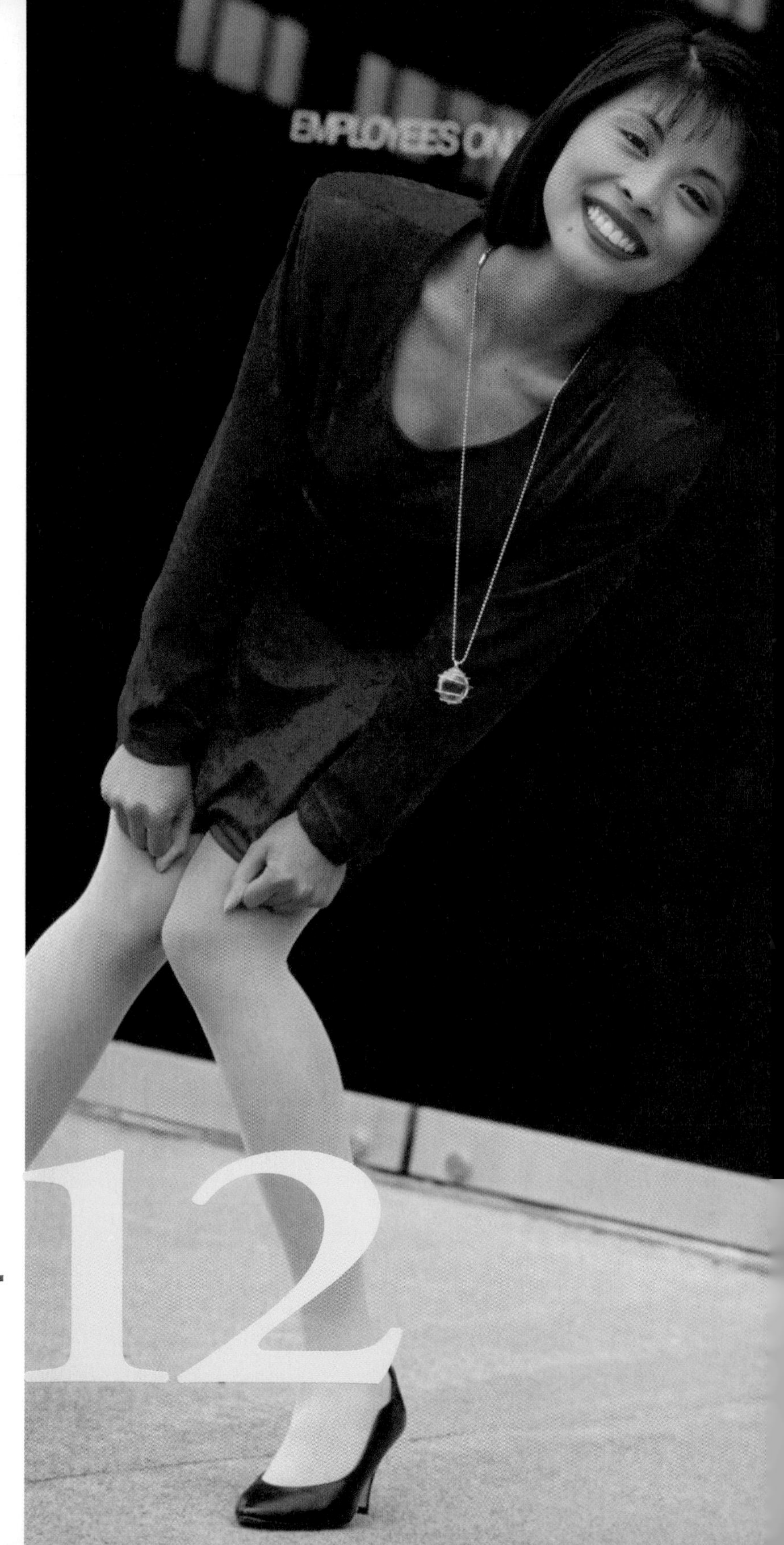

Chapter 12

Lifestyle Essentials

You have devoted time to the cultivation and strengthening of your inner resources through good health practices, relaxation techniques and beauty rituals. Now it's time to create conditions in your outer life that provide the same kind of support for your soul.

We are most at peace when our inner and outer lives are in harmony. As you learn to listen more to your inner voice, you will begin to have a much clearer understanding of who you are and what you prefer. Your personality and preferences will come into sharper focus. You will become attuned to what makes you happy and what supports your inner being.

The places we live, the jobs we accept, the people with whom we surround ourselves—all have a tremendous impact on our well-being. Invest the energy to find a job that nourishes and supports your being and makes use of your special gifts. Balance your work with time devoted to play, laughter and cultivating creativity. We need these things in our lives as a source of joy and lightness. Relationships play such a large role in our peace of mind that it's important to consider these carefully too. Finally, set aside time in your busy life to care for your spirit, the real source of your inner beauty.

Job Satisfaction

Everyone has their own requirements for work. Some seek only a steady paycheck and regular hours, especially when occupied with other demanding tasks, such as raising children. For others, the challenge of a career is as satisfying and important as the paycheck. A few consider their work such an intrinsic part of their lives that their profession is not merely what they do, but who they are.

Because our jobs demand so much of our time, being happy in them makes a big difference in our lives. The better you understand what you seek from a job, the more apt you are to find one that suits you. Start the exploration process by answering the questions on the "Rate Your Job" form.

After you have answered these questions for yourself, think about how your answers relate to the career you are pursuing. Does the job you are seeking make use of your technical skills, which are your strength, or does it require that you spend most of your time in meetings? Does your current workplace provide the cooperative atmosphere that allows you do to your best work, or does it require that you compete against other employees?

If you find that your skills and preferences match the career choice you have made, congratulations! If not, consider whether you might be happier in another job. You may not even need to change employers; a different position in the same company might be enough of an adjustment.

For example, let's say you are a physical therapist working in a hospital. You are good with patients, but find that you're happiest when performing administrative tasks and organizing programs and people. Instead of trying to change yourself to fit the job, why not change the job to fit you? A move into management would allow you to use your talents to their fullest.

Getting the Scoop

When you're considering a new career, one of the best ways to learn more about what's actually involved in a job is to conduct informational interviews with people who are employed in the profession. Contact people who have jobs similar to the one you are considering or who supervise those who do. Ask if they would be willing to meet with you for twenty minutes. Make it clear you are not seeking employment with them at this time, but just want to learn about the job. Go into the interview with a list of questions you would like answered. The answers you get will help you focus your job search more realistically.

A career counselor can be of help in evaluating your skills and pinpointing job opportunities that would be appropriate. Friends and family may also have ideas to offer, as they observe you in different situations and know many of your strengths and abilities.

To know what you prefer instead of humbly saying 'Amen' to what the world tells you you ought to prefer, is to have kept your soul alive.

—Robert Louis Stevenson, Author

Rate Your Job

How important is work in your life at this time?________________________

Where does it rank with your family, social life, hobbies and personal growth?____________

Do you prefer working closely with others or by yourself?____________________

Does your strength lie in your social, analytical, manual, technical or artistic abilities?________

Do you work best in a cooperative or a competitive situation?____________________

Are you a natural organizer or do you thrive on "creative chaos"?__________________

Do you enjoy responsibility or do you prefer to follow orders?___________________

Do you prefer a great deal of flexibility and freedom or does a feeling of security inspire your best efforts?______________________________

Do you like to travel for work or stay close to home?____________________

Do you prefer to communicate your ideas in a written report or by speaking publicly?

Do you need a lot of encouragement and praise or are you self-sufficient?

Do you gain satisfaction from helping others?

Do you like producing a tangible product?

Do you enjoy being around glamour and excitement?

Do you like being in the spotlight or working behind the scenes?

Is attaining recognition, power and authority important to you?

What kind of a salary and benefits do you desire?

What kind of work schedule do you prefer?

When you are doing the work you love, all else in life seems to fall into place.

—Nancy Anderson, Writer

Time for Everything

"There's not enough time in the day!" we often lament. The problem may not be that there's too little time in the day, but that we're wasting too much of it on unimportant tasks and not leaving enough for the things that really matter.

How do spend your time? To find out, keep a log of your activities for a few days. Write down everything you do and how long you spend doing it. Add up the time you spend on each of the categories and fill in the blanks below.

At Home	Weekday	Weekend Day
Cooking	________	________
Eating	________	________
Sleep and Naps	________	________
Grooming	________	________
Dressing	________	________
Sex	________	________
Care of Children	________	________
Errands	________	________
Housekeeping	________	________
Commuting	________	________
Daydreaming	________	________
Meditation/Relaxing	________	________
Sports/Exercise	________	________
Television	________	________
Reading	________	________
Telephone	________	________
Conversation	________	________
Culture/Arts	________	________
Hobbies	________	________
Volunteer Work	________	________
Clubs and Church	________	________

At Work

Meetings	________
Socializing	________
Telephone Calls	________
Lunch	________
Routine Matters	________
Low Priority Items	________
Productive Work	________

Are you devoting enough time to the things you really want and need to do? Or are you wasting time on relatively unimportant activities? If your time diary shows that you are not using your time as well as you could, follow these guidelines.

Start a "to do" list. In a notebook or on a computer file, write down your everyday maintenance tasks, such as laundry and bill-paying, as well as the larger goals you wish to achieve, such as buying a new house. Separate and prioritize items that need to be done today, this week and beyond.

Eliminate unnecessary tasks and those that can be delegated to other people. Then set deadlines for the items that remain and estimate the time needed to complete them. Update your list frequently, and cross off tasks as you complete them.

Intimate Ties • From the moment we are born, we begin to form attachments. Each new environment we enter—family, school, neighborhood, social gatherings, work—brings us into contact with new acquaintances. As we grow up, these connections increase and overlap. We meet someone in college who later becomes a coworker who eventually introduces us to the person we marry. The social safety net we have woven over the years provides the support that we need in both happy and trying times.

Medical researchers say people with social ties live longer and are healthier than those who are without them. People who are married or have close relationships with friends and family benefit most, but even those who draw support from a church or social group are protected.

Sometimes we need to increase our circle of acquaintances and bring more intimates into our life. But how do you go about doing it? Get involved with a group, club or class where you can easily meet other people. Invite those you like to go out for coffee or dinner so you can get better acquainted. Build the friendships you already have by staying in touch regularly by telephone, e-mail, letters and visits.

You grow up the day you have your *first* real laugh at yourself.
—*Ethel Barrymore, Actor*

Be sure that the attachments you build are healthy ones. Treat yourself with respect and insist that others do the same. Say "no" when you want or need to, even if it means displeasing other people. Taking care of yourself is just as important as ministering to the needs of other people.

Love and Sexuality • Sex is the most profoundly intimate experience we share with another person. It is an expression of our feelings about ourselves and our partners. It is a celebration of our sensual natures, expressed through touch, taste, sight, sound and smell. It can be playful, exciting, healing and even humorous. It is an affirmation of our beings.

Our ability to give and receive pleasure is proportionate to our ability to be "in the moment"—free of worry and self-consciousness. This means accepting and appreciating our bodies, and resisting media-imposed ideas of what a "perfect" body should look like. Allow yourself to take pleasure in your body by respecting your own specialness and beauty. Remember that sexuality is not just about how we look—it is the totality of our whole being.

Confidence is a turn-on. A woman who accepts herself and takes pleasure in her body is sexually attractive. If you are less than comfortable with your sensual being, nurture this side of yourself. Get massages, go to a spa and be pampered. Learn to enjoy your own body and discover what brings you the most pleasure. If you would like to know more about how to please yourself and your partner sexually, educate yourself. Allow yourself to enjoy and appreciate your God-given right to sensual pleasure.

Remember that you are in charge of your sexuality. A sexual experience should always be on *your* terms. Don't let yourself be coerced into doing what you don't want to do, and don't do anything you don't really enjoy. Be gentle and loving with yourself in expressing your sexuality, as in everything else.

Laughter & Play

A sense of wonder and play are things we easily enjoy in childhood. As adults, we often leave these behind, thinking they are unimportant or beneath us. But we need a balance of work and play in our lives. Laughter, joy and sheer silliness are as worthwhile as any serious endeavor.

The ability to laugh at ourselves and life's absurdities in a loving manner is a sign of emotional strength and maturity. It takes a healthy dose of self-esteem to see the humor in our own faults and quirky traits. Medical researchers believe that the ability to find humor in life may even help us live longer. When an uncomfortable sentiment is expressed in comedic terms, our laughter provides a release for our emotions and the tension of the moment.

If you're not used to looking at life in a humorous manner, start opening your eyes to see the comedy in situations. When things get too serious or mundane, tell a joke or do something utterly silly. In doing so, you will begin to enjoy life more and increase others' enjoyment as well.

Living Creatively • Creativity is not the exclusive province of artists, musicians and writers. Each one of us has the ability to be creative. Creativity is defined as showing artistic or intellectual inventiveness. To live creatively is to be willing to try new ways of doing things when the old ways no longer serve our needs. Creativity can be applied to every aspect of our lives—jobs, relationships, homes and hobbies.

What if you are a bookkeeper or a lab technician? In professions such as these, accuracy and consistency are critical, and creativity is not often appropriate. Still, every job has some room for creativity. Perhaps you've found a procedure that is inefficient and need to think of a better way to get it done. Or perhaps you want to figure out how to approach your coworkers to get more cooperation or come up with a new system for organizing your files. Each one of these situations requires creative thinking.

If you haven't been as creative as you would like, you can begin now. Cultivate creativity as you would any other skill—by practice. Let's say you are looking for a more efficient way to process invoices. Start by framing the problem—write it down, so it's very clear. Now do your research. Think about all the ways invoices might be handled, talk to other people to get their ideas, read manuals for suggestions and gather as much information as you can. When you're done, review your findings thoroughly and then put them aside. Give yourself time to assimilate the information; let it percolate and simmer inside you. Don't try too hard to come up with an answer—a relaxed mind is usually best for stimulating creativity. Ideas pop up unexpectedly, while taking a shower, driving to work, washing dishes and doing other repetitive or mundane tasks.

Don't fall into the habit of always doing something one way just because that's the way it's always been done. Take a different route to work now and then. Eat lunch in the restaurant you've passed by every day for the last five years. Read a political magazine whose philosophy is the opposite of your own. Look at life as an adventure in which you can experiment, succeed, fail, learn and grow.

Creativity comes from considering fresh possibilities and new ways of seeing

Creativity *is oxygen for the soul.*

—Julia Cameron, Writer

things. It requires an open mind and a willingness to wait for the best solution, rather than rushing toward the easy one.

Feeding the Spirit • Daily life keeps us swirling in a sea of activities, relationships, conflicts and change. It's difficult to find perspective in the middle of it all. Quiet, meditative times allow us to step back and put life into perspective. Only then are we able to see the pattern of the "whole," and our place within it.

Traditionally we have tended to our spiritual needs by participating in church and temple services. The ritualistic aspect of these services is part of their appeal and value. As we walk through the doors of our chosen house of worship, the music, the people and the setting trigger a response in us that is almost automatic. It takes us into a reflective state and allows us to shift gears out of our active lives more easily than we might otherwise be able to do on our own.

Some people feel a strong spiritual connection when they are outdoors—hiking on a nature trail, walking on the beach or around a lake, even strolling through a park or garden. There is something very comforting about witnessing the order of nature, the cyclical changes in plant and animal life as the seasons go by, and the interrelatedness of every life form. We are released from our self-centered state to see that life thrives all around us and that we too fit into this grand design.

I am not afraid of storms for I am learning how to sail my ship.

—Louisa May Alcott, Author

This primal force—call it God, nature, the universe, a higher power—is the source of energy and consciousness. We are completely dependent on it for life itself. This vast, complex natural order gives us the food we eat, the air we breathe, the warming energy of the sun. The life force that flows through every other living thing flows through us as well. We have only to open up and receive it.

This is what gives us our strength and inner peace: the knowledge that we are not isolated, not alone, but part of a larger order that is limitless and self-sustaining. We are connected to everything and everyone around us. All is right with us, because we are right with the world. Our balance is restored.

A Perfect Day

So much of our time is devoted to meeting obligations, taking care of responsibilities and maintaining mindless routines. No wonder we sometimes feel we are just slogging through our lives, putting one foot in front of the other each day just to keep going.

What if you had a day free in which you could do anything you like, with no "shoulds" or "musts" to occupy you? What would you do? Would you putter around the house, shop, take a ceramics class, stay in bed and read, scuba dive, give a dinner party or catch up on some work? Would you want to be with other people or use the time to do something by yourself? Sketch out a picture of your perfect day, writing down everything you would do from the moment you got up in the morning until the time you went to bed at night.

Chapter 13

Beauty Shared

The final step in the unfolding of your inner beauty involves sharing it with others. You are not content to just display yourself to be admired by others, for you have so much more to give. Your beauty is compelling, vital and dynamic. You want to interact with the world, share your gifts and fulfill your promise.

There are many different ways in which you can give back to your family, your community, your world. Giving doesn't require only grand gestures—you can share your beauty everyday through small acts of kindness. The first step is to be an active, positive

force in your world. You can strive in all your dealings to be fair and honorable, treating other people as you would like to be treated. Then if you have the time (and the inclination), you can also give to those you don't know by volunteering time with a community organization or donating to a worthy cause. When you give to those outside of your immediate circle, you expand your sense of community and become a richer human being.

It's because you have learned how to take care of yourself that you are able to give to others. You've learned the importance of giving from a full cup. Never forget to take care of yourself first. Stay aware of your own inner feelings and give when you feel comfortable doing so. Care for yourself as much you would for a dear friend.

When you are generous and compassionate with yourself, you will naturally treat others in the same manner. You will not be giving out of a need to get anything back from others, but as an expression of your inner beauty and your personal power. You have come into your own and have much to share with the world.

Benefits of Giving •

When you give with no strings attached, your giving will always be rewarded. It may not be returned to you from the same source or in the same way, but return it will. For when you live your life in a generous, open manner, you create a positive dynamic that inspires the goodwill of others. When you help others, your health even improves. One study of people who volunteered their time to worthy causes found that nine out of ten people were healthier than those who didn't volunteer. Another study showed that those who donate their time to helping other people even live longer.

Your world becomes larger when you take other people's needs into consideration. When we give of ourselves, we become intimately connected with other people. For example, after a church meeting you might offer to give someone you don't know very well a ride home. Along the way, you get to know each other and soon it's the beginning of a new friendship. Our lives seem to hold a greater purpose when we are helping someone else: We've broken out of the prison of self-involvement, which ultimately leads to loneliness.

Getting involved with others is the best cure for loneliness and depression. When we see that others also share many of the same feelings and experiences, we don't feel so alone. When we spend time helping those who are disadvantaged, poor or troubled, it puts our own struggles in better perspective. And when we help others, we inspire a feeling of gratitude in them. It's uplifting to be seen by another person in this positive light. And it makes us feel good to know we have done something good for another person and have made a difference in the world.

It is a healing experience to help someone else who is struggling with something that you yourself have mastered, whether it involves learning a new skill or overcoming adversity. Seeing others in similar positions as yourself—and sharing their experiences—prompts memories of where you were before and how far you have come. In many twelve-step programs, becoming a mentor for a new member is one of the first steps in recovery. Such groups recognize that by helping others work toward a goal of sobriety, not gambling or not overeating, mentors can recommit themselves to their own recovery.

Giving to others can be a way of honoring those who once gave to us. Each of us owes some measure of our success to the kindness and assistance of others. Remember the high school coach who looked out for you and made you feel like you

Unless you choose to do great things with it, it makes no difference how much you are rewarded, or how much power you have.

—Oprah Winfrey, Talk show host

were someone special? . . . the teacher who encouraged you to excel, then wrote a glowing letter of recommendation? . . . the "big sister" who took you under her wing? . . . the mentor on your first job who set you on the right course? You can pay back these debts, not necessarily by giving back to the same people who helped you, but by giving to someone else who could use your help. In this way, you too continue the cycle of giving.

Everyday Acts • Sometimes the littlest actions make the biggest difference of all. Even if you don't have time for a volunteer commitment, or money for charitable giving, you can adopt an attitude of generosity in your everyday life.

You influence the lives of so many people in the course of a day. When you give a big smile and a friendly greeting to the receptionist at your office, it can turn her day around. And that has an effect on all the people she later comes into contact with, for now she's friendlier to them too. Those people experience her friendliness and feel better. And they pass it on. It's amazing how much one smile can do for the world.

Kind words can be short and easy to speak, but their echoes are truly endless.
—Mother Teresa, Missionary to the poor

You may not realize how big a role you play in other people's lives. Your elderly neighbor next door may get a big boost out of your energy, enthusiasm and friendly attitude and look forward to seeing you each day. The little girl with the troubled family down the street may look up to you as someone she admires. Give them a few minutes of your time now and then, and it can have a profound impact on their lives (and yours as well).

Think back to people in your own life who have made a big impression on you. Often they were people you didn't even know very well or spend much time with. But twenty years later you still remember that day when your friend's older sister gave you the compliment on your art project that made you feel so good. Or you may still be ashamed about the snide remark someone made that you'll never forget because it hit so close to home.

Take the time to treat people in your life with care. Smile at that elderly neighbor walking past your house in the morning. Allow yourself an extra five minutes for the commute to work so you can let other drivers have the right of way occasionally. Treat service people with courtesy and respect. Send a funny postcard to friends with a message of appreciation. Take a moment out of your morning rush to say some kind words to your son or daughter. (This will give both of you a good start on the day!) Keep your temper on a long leash when you encounter irritating people and situations.

Behaving in this manner is like keeping your house clean. It's an act of self care as much as it is the "right" thing to do. After all, you're the one who lives in the house, and you know how much more pleasant it is to live in a clean house than one that is cluttered and dirty.

Community Ties • Our communities are only as strong as their weakest members. By strengthening those who are more vulnerable, we build up the strength of our communities as a whole, and everyone benefits.

For example, what happens when children in at-risk family situations have no parks to play in, no after-school programs, no caring adults who really take an interest in their welfare? They may turn instead to criminal activity. This outcome not only hurts them, their families and neighborhoods, it hurts those of us in the larger community. Slowly, crime rates increase and we feel less safe in our homes and on our streets.

But instead of standing by helplessly and bemoaning society's problems, we can roll up our sleeves and do something positive to help solve them. We can feel powerful, rather than powerless. It's a sign of our strength when we are able to reach out and help someone else up. The act of reaching out to help someone we don't know is reassuring as well. We are reminded that we too will be taken care of and helped daily by the "kindness of strangers."

Be A Mentor

Want to make a difference? Consider becoming a mentor. A study of teenagers in the Big Brothers/Big Sisters program shows that kids who meet regularly with their volunteer mentors do better in school and have better relationships with their parents and peers. Having a mentor also dramatically decreases drug and alcohol use in youths.

Even the smallest actions can help us feel connected to our communities. Become active in a parents' group at your children's school. Participate in a walk-a-thon to raise money for a community hospital. Organize a block party and get to know your neighbors. Buy the raffle tickets and candy bars that kids are always selling to benefit their school or team, and be friendly and kind to them when you do. Look out for the elderly woman who lives next door and offer her a ride to the grocery store now and then.

Corporations and companies can contribute to their communities too. For example, as part of a community-building effort, Freeman Cosmetics moved its manufacturing plant back into an inner city section of Los Angeles at a time when many existing companies in the area were looking to the suburbs and overseas for their manufacturing work forces. As a company, Freeman Cosmetics believes it can benefit the community by adding new jobs and tax revenue to a depressed area. Perhaps there would have been fewer risks in locating to another area, but communities are shaped by individual decisions such as these. We are part of our community in both good times *and* bad, and we try to contribute in whatever way we can. It's simply not enough to complain about a problem and then turn away.

We can get more involved in our communities in both small and large ways. Being a contributing, positive member of the community means that you make your decisions with the rest of the community in mind. But what is good for the community is good for you too.

The Volunteer Solution • One of the best ways we can give to the world is by volunteering with a nonprofit or charitable organization. There are so many deserving organizations in need of volunteers and so much we can do to help. It's amazing how much difference just a few hours of our time each week can make to an organization.

In addition to being a positive force for the larger community, volunteering can expose us to worlds we may not otherwise encounter. It can enrich our lives, help us gain new skills and open us

Before You Volunteer

What kind of volunteer assignment is best for you? Answer these questions to help pinpoint what type of volunteer effort would be the best match for you.

Are you available for ongoing, regularly scheduled work? Or would you prefer to donate time on a project basis now and then? ____________________

____

How much time do you have to give? A day or more each week? A few hours a week? One day a month? A few hours a month? ____________________

____

Are you available days? Evenings? Weekends? ____________________

____

Do you prefer to work by yourself, one-on-one or with groups of people? ____________________

____

Do you prefer to work in an office? Outdoors? At home? In a public setting, such as a school, hospital or library? ____________________

____

Do you have equipment to share, such as use of a car or a home computer? ____________________

____

What kind of group in need would you like to assist (elderly, the environment, women)? ____________________

____

Would you prefer a large, established organization or a casual, smaller operation? ____________________

____

Would you rather help society's needy (homeless, runaways) or a civic or arts organization that contributes to the community as a whole (Junior League, museum docents, gardening club?) ____________________

____

What skills would you like to contribute? ____________________

____

What skills would you like to improve or acquire? ____________________

____

Would you like to take on a great deal of independent responsibility or would you prefer to have very defined tasks? ____________________

____

Do you want to use this experience to help you in the work world? ____________________

____

What would you like to get out of the experience? ____________________

____

Volunteer Opportunities

The opportunities for volunteer work are much broader than you might think. Here are just some of the types of organizations or groups that can *always* use volunteer help.

- Food banks
- Health clinics
- Disaster relief organizations
- Mentoring programs
- Homeless shelters
- Church programs
- Political campaigns
- Disease research
- Hospices and hospitals
- Legal protection agencies
- Alcohol and drug rehabilitation
- Translation services
- Museums
- Public gardens and parks
- Wilderness groups
- Girl Scouts/Boy Scouts
- Crisis hot lines
- Youth or disabled sports teams
- Recreational programs
- AIDS prevention
- Elder care
- Literacy programs
- Parenting education
- Rape counseling
- Community policing
- Neighborhood watch
- Laboratory volunteer
- CPR instructor
- Nature clubs
- Tutoring services
- Child advocacy
- Foster parenting
- 12-step support groups
- Nonprofit resale shops
- Meal delivery to shut-ins
- Special Olympics
- AIDS organizations
- Women's health organizations
- Battered women shelters
- Hunger relief
- Peace Corps/Vista
- Volunteer clearinghouses
- Red Cross
- Habitat for Humanity
- Big Brothers/Big Sisters
- Performance (theater, opera, musical) groups
- Animal rescue
- Recycling centers
- Church outreach
- Community computer centers

Most Needed

Want to give where the need for assistance is most critical? Studies of community needs have targeted these top priorities.

- Children and teens at risk
- Support for the elderly
- HIV/AIDS
- Adult literacy
- Health education and research
- Physical and sexual abuse
- Substance abuse
- Homelessness

up to new experiences. Volunteering doesn't always mean just stuffing envelopes or answering telephones. You can join a ski rescue patrol or lead an amateur theater group for disadvantaged youths, coach a sport for the disabled or help build homes for low-income families. You may be donating your time when you volunteer, but the work you do doesn't have to be a grind. In fact, the more you enjoy the job, the more successful your volunteer experience will be.

Is there an issue or cause that is close to your heart? A societal concern that really pushes your buttons? Do something about it by volunteering. If you have a soft spot in your heart for children who have had a rough start in life, you can volunteer with a program for disadvantaged youths. Perhaps you are concerned about the incidence of breast cancer among women. In this case you might want to do some work for an agency that raises money for cancer research. Maybe you'd like to get more politically involved and would enjoy serving on a local campaign or committee.

Match Skills to Needs • What type of volunteer job should you seek? You can contribute the valuable skills you already have, perhaps one that you use already in your paid work. Organizations are always grateful for the services of real pros, whether they involve fundraising, newsletter design or computer programming.

You may decide that you want to do something completely different from what you normally do during the day. If you have a desk job, for example, you may enjoy a volunteer job that is more physical or that requires working outdoors. If you work out of your home, so that your ordinary work activities are fairly solitary, you can choose a volunteer job that brings you into closer contact with other people. If you want to learn a new skill, such as teaching or using computers, you can look for volunteer efforts involving these activities.

Choose a volunteer organization with the same care you would give to choosing your paying job. Talk with at least a few different agencies. Ask about their programs and goals and the role that volunteers play in the organization. Visit the agency you are interested in before making a time commitment. This will give you a feeling for the staff, the people being served and the working environment. Be clear with the agency in describing exactly what you can contribute and what you want to achieve from the experience.

Finding an Organization • Once you've determined the type of work you want to do, it just takes a little detective work to find the right organization. You may find what

Finding An Organization

Here is a sampling of nonprofit organizations that use volunteers. Call to get information about local chapters or offices.

The Arts

American Association of Museum Volunteers
1225 I St., N.W.
Suite 200
Washington, D.C. 20005
202/289-6575

Children/Youth

Big Brothers/Big Sisters of America
230 North Thirteenth St.
Philadelphia, PA 19107
215/567-7000

Girl Scouts of America
420 Fifth Ave.
New York, NY 10018
212/852-8000

Community Service

U.S. Americorps/VISTA
1201 New York Ave., N.W.
Washington, D.C. 20525
800/942-2677

The Disabled

Special Olympics International
1325 G St., N.W.
Suite 500
Washington, D.C. 20005
202/628-3630

Education

National Association of Partners in Education
601 Wythe St.
Suite 200
Alexandria, VA 22314
703/836-4880

The Elderly

Foster Grandparent Program
1100 Vermont Ave., N.W.
6th Floor
Washington, D.C. 20525
202/678-4215

The Environment

Sierra Club
730 Polk St.
San Francisco, CA 94109
415/776-2211

The Nature Conservancy
1815 N. Lynn St.
Arlington, VA 22209
703/841-5300

Disaster Relief

American Red Cross
Disaster Services
43 East Ohio
Chicago, IL 60611
312/440-2039

Health Care

American Red Cross
Office of HIV/AIDS Education
1709 New York Ave., N.W.
Washington, D.C. 20006
703/206-7130

National Hospice Organization
1901 N. Moore St.
Suite 901
Arlington, VA 22209
800/646-6460

Housing
Habitat for Humanity International
419 W. Church St.
Americus, GA 31709
912/924-6935

Hunger and Poverty
Friends of the Third World
611 W. Wayne St.
Ft. Wayne, IN 46802
219/422-6821

Literacy
Coalition for Literacy
50 E. Huron St.
Chicago, IL 60611
312/944-6780

Physical Fitness Education
YMCA of the U.S.A.
101 North Wacker Dr.
Chicago, IL 60606
312/269-0512

Volunteer Clearinghouses
International Christian Youth Exchange
134 W. 26th St.
New York, NY 10001
212/206-7307

Points of Light Foundation
1737 H St., N.W.
Washington, D.C. 20006
800/879-5400

United Way of America
701 N. Fairfax Ave.
Alexandria, VA 22314
703/836-7100

Internet Sites

You can also find information about many volunteer opportunities electronically. Given the growth of the Internet in the past couple of years, your community volunteer clearinghouse may already have its own site on the 'net. Here are some listings of Internet sites that provide information on volunteering efforts and opportunities both nationwide and worldwide.

The Internet Nonprofit Center provides free access to information on nonprofit organizations, wise giving practices and issues of concern to donors and volunteers. http://www.human.com:80/inc/

The Contact Center Network has a directory of volunteer, nonprofit and charitable organizations on the Internet with links to more than 3,000 sites organized by issue and geography. It promotes community-based Contact Centers to help individuals and organizations build a sense of community. http://www.contact.org/

Nonprofit Organizations on the Internet lists more than sixty organizations, from the ACLU to World Conservation. gopher://www.ai.mit.edu:80/hGET %20/people/ellens/non.html

National and International Volunteering Information lists environmentally related jobs, internships, field research expeditions, voluntary organizations and general volunteer information. gopher://gopher.igc.apc.org:70/00/orgs/ran/volunteer

Impact Online is a new nonprofit organization that is helping people get involved with nonprofit organizations nationwide through the use of technology. http://www.webcom.com/~iol/

The Institute for Global Communications publishes a directory of environmental and community organizations and resources. http://www.igc.apc.org/

Global Volunteers offers worldwide volunteer service programs with the goal of building world peace through service to others. http://www.globalvlntrs.org/globalvol/gvhome.htm

International Volunteer Projects (CIEE) provides short-term volunteer opportunities for individuals who would like to do environmental or community service work as part of an international team. http://www.ciee.org:80/vol/ivphome.htm

you're looking for in telephone listings. Newspapers are another good reference. Most newspapers have a regular feature that describes a wide variety of volunteer opportunities that are available in your community. You may also read an article about a local group that interests you. Give them a call to see if they use volunteers.

Your employer may be a good source of leads. Many employers encourage their employees to volunteer in their communities and have established relationships with local organizations. Contact your company's human affairs or human resources office for suggestions.

Just about every state has a governor's office of volunteerism that provides referrals. And most big cities have volunteer centers, which will not only give you leads, but also help you determine what type of organization best fits your needs, interests and abilities.

Make A Commitment • Decide ahead of time how much time you can easily commit, and then be sure to stick to it. Start with a small commitment and only increase your time later when you are ready. Many organizations have great needs for volunteer help. If you say yes to everything you will soon be overwhelmed. Give only what is comfortable, otherwise you will burn out early and want to quit, which does neither you nor the organization any good. Keep in mind that volunteer work doesn't have to be an ongoing commitment. It can be the willingness to get involved now and then when an issue comes to the fore. For example, a decision by the school board looks like it will adversely affect your children and others at their school: Get involved and lobby against it. Your company is participating in a walk-a-thon to benefit a charitable organization: Get a couple of coworkers to join you and participate in the walk.

If you do take on a regular volunteer assignment, make sure you have a job description and an open line of communication with your volunteer supervisor. Meet with that person regularly to discuss your work. Are you being used well, or do you spend too much time waiting around? Is there something else you'd rather be doing? Are there any conflicts with staff or clients that you need help in resolving? These are the kinds of things a volunteer supervisor or coordinator can—and should—help you with.

If the job doesn't appear to be working out or is not what you thought it would be, let the agency know and relinquish your assignment. There are so many different volunteer opportunities that you will eventually find one that is just right for you. Enthusiasm for the work is most important. When you do work that you believe in, giving will seem like no effort at all.

The dedicated life is the life worth living.

—Annie Dillard, Writer

INDEX

ABOUT THE AUTHORS • Jill Freeman is Director of Marketing for Freeman Cosmetics Corporation. She is both a charming and confident young woman who has grown up working with her father Larry for Freeman Cosmetics. At 30, Jill is the embodiment of the book's philosophy. Judged too "old" by Madison Avenue's standards, she proves that mentality wrong by modeling in Freeman's television commercials. "I'm better looking now than I was at 18," Jill says. And she has applied this forthright self-confidence to the content of this book.

Within Freeman Cosmetics and with respect to this book, Jill Freeman provides a valuable symmetry to Larry's vision, reflecting the views and feelings of today's generation of women. This father and daughter collaboration, providing the all-important balance of male and female perspectives, has added real dynamism and depth to *Your Inner Beauty*.

Larry J. Freeman, CEO of Freeman Cosmetics Corporation, is photogenic, talented, and immensely successful. He is widely recognized in the United States and Canada because he has hosted his own syndicated television show, "Larry Freeman's Women's Page"; he has been widely interviewed on other television shows; his picture is included in most of his company's print advertising; and his signature appears on every cosmetics bottle, tube and jar his company sells.

Moreover, Larry Freeman is truly an expert in all aspects of the beauty business. He was born into a family immersed in it. He earned a degree at UCLA, then went to work at Clairol, where he became expert in hair care and coloring products. In 1961, he joined the family business. In 1976, he combined his marketing and business experience with his fresh ideas on cosmetic formulation to reorganize the business into the Freeman Cosmetic Corporation. His goal was to produce unique, top quality personal care treatments formulated with natural ingredients.